JOURNEY

—

A PATH TO BIBLICAL CHANGE

LAURA CHICA

Made to Minister Training
375 Madrona Ave. S
Salem, OR 97302

CONTENTS

APPENDICES

Charts

Resources

CONTRIBUTORS

Laura Chica has a pastor husband, four incredible adult children, one amazing teenager, two beloved sons-in-law, and a pack of labradoodles she calls her family. She is a popular and much-loved biblical counselor in Salem, Oregon and serves as the Director of Women's Biblical Counseling at Salem Heights Church. Laura uses her great passion and love for women to walk with them as they learn how to take joy in the personal narrative story God is writing in their lives. She is a sought-after speaker for women's events and also is an instructor in training biblical counselors.

Carl Chica is a pastor at Salem Heights Church. He oversees the biblical counseling ministry and the Made to Minister training for biblical counseling and community education. He teaches in a variety of church and conference settings, serves as an adjunct instructor at Corban University and provides biblical counseling to individuals and families. Carl holds a Master's Degree in Marriage, Family and Child counseling from California State University. He and his wife, Laura, have five children. They enjoy ministering together as counselors and training pastors in how to care for their congregations.

1

Justin Greene has led us in our mission to reach our community with the gospel of Jesus Christ since accepting the role of senior pastor in September 2008. He began attending Salem Heights in September 1992. Eager to get involved, he started serving part-time in youth ministry in January of the following year and transitioned to full-time ministry in January 1996. In 2005, he began co-leading as associate pastor until making the full transition to senior pastor three years later. He and his wife, Christina, have been married since 1992 and have three children.

Chara Donahue enjoys freelance writing, biblical counseling, and speaking to women when her four kids are out playing with dad. She holds an MSEd from Corban University and is passionate about seeing people set free through God's truths. She is a regular contributor at iBelieve, and her words have appeared at Christianity Today, Crosswalk, (in)courage, and The Huffington Post. It has been her greatest honor to do her best to serve Jesus, and it has been a privilege to work with others trying to do the same.

Emily Dempster serves as a biblical counselor and the Made to Minister training coordinator at Salem Heights Church in Salem, Oregon. She has a deep passion to see women defined not by their circumstances but by who they were created to be. Compelled by her passion for God's Word and discipleship in the local church she works hard at counseling and encouraging women, and developing curriculum to be used in the discipleship process. She earned her Master of Arts in Pastoral Counseling from Liberty University Theological Seminary. Married since 1998 to Ryan, they have two children.

Doreen (Sam) Button became staff editor for Randy Alcorn/ Eternal Perspective Ministries in 2008. Many years and millions of words later, she finds herself also happily working alongside the wonderful counseling staff at Salem Heights to birth this excellent curriculum. Watching, and sometimes aiding in people's lives becoming transformed by God's healing truth, energizes her as she works for the "Well done!"

INTRODUCTION

————

Chances are, you have found yourself in the midst of crisis and suffering and are reaching out for resources, input, support and direction—after all, healthy people seek help. In life's journey, you've come to recognize that you do not have the capacity or means to alleviate or resolve your suffering. You may find yourself feeling hopeless, depressed, anxious, regretful, angry, lacking peace and joy. You hold on to the idea that *if* someone could help alleviate your problems, difficult relationships, or circumstances, you just might finally enjoy the life God has for you.

What if the Bible presented a radically different view of trial and difficulty? What if your current suffering is actually the means to the joy and peace you so desire, and that God so longs for you to experience? What if you could truly consider it all joy when you face trials because you know that the outcome would bring you into a deeper relationship with the living God? What if Jesus was actually the treasure, the end game, the prize that you sought, and what if suffering was the path that would bring you into closer relationship with Him? Would you still want to follow Him?

Would temporary suffering be a worthwhile exchange for the lasting peace and happiness God promises? Would you open your heart completely to God's wonderful plan for your life even if it includes pain and suffering?

We often raise a hand to accept Jesus into our lives because we believe He will bring blessing, prosperity, friendship, alleviation of pain, ease and comfort. But being a follower of Jesus is actually not a guarantee of the elimination of our experiences of brokenness and suffering, but following Him may even increase them. Jesus said that He alone is life and a relationship with Him is worth giving up all the things this world has to offer and the suffering we incur while living in it.

Consider how Jesus lived in relationship with His disciples. He called them to follow Him as He led them across stormy seas, life threatening close calls, persecution, their personal failures and ultimately his humiliating and horrifying death on the cross. Their journey with Jesus was challenging, unpredictable and radically different from what they anticipated. He did and said astounding things that broke cultural norms and religious expectations continually. These things stretched and pushed the disciples out of a comfortable and predictable life. They found that His thoughts and His ways were so radically different from their own. Real-life experiences and suffering taught them, over and over again, who He was and modeled for them how they should live. Jesus exemplified for them a life lived out in dependence and obedience to the Father in all things. He taught them to trust and follow Him even when they were overwhelmed, confused, tired, hungry and afraid.

Throughout each day, Jesus orchestrated circumstances and relational opportunities for His disciples' spiritual growth. He used the everyday context of life to teach them what it means to bear His image, His love, patience, peace, gentleness, kindness, and self-control in a broken world. He used the challenging circumstances and relationships to accomplish all that He desired to bring them to maturity in their faith.

In the middle of difficulties and suffering, Jesus continued to reveal Himself to them and to reveal their hearts to themselves.

Through difficulty and trial He brought to the surface their self-oriented desires and fears and how those desires and fears drove their thinking and their actions. He used each circumstance to reveal their faith, where they were trusting Him and where they were still dependent on themselves. God longs to do the same for us on our journey of biblical change.

Jesus says, if you want to follow Me you must deny yourself (all that you desire and all that you fear) and pick up your cross (a picture of suffering and death) and follow Me wherever I may lead (Luke 9:23). Is following Jesus even in suffering what you signed up for? Because it just might be the answer to what you are seeking. *Suffering is part of the journey of biblical change and growth.*

On this journey, we will start by laying a solid foundation of biblical truth that will establish our steps as we, like the disciples, follow our savior, Jesus.

On this journey you will learn to recognize how God is working to disclose what your heart is determined to disguise: your own self-rule.

This journey will also reveal who you believe God is and whose kingdom you are building, defending and living for.

This journey will reveal who is charting the course through your life…you or God. Are you leaning on your own understanding or depending on and trusting in Him to direct your path?

You will come to recognize that you live behind enemy lines and that your greatest battle is not with others but is truly a spiritual battle meant to keep you from fixing your eyes on the one you follow, Jesus.

This journey will reveal that how you think about suffering greatly effects how suffering impacts you.

The disciples' call to follow Jesus was tangible, it happened in real time in their own lives. However, our call to follow Jesus on the journey is just as real though not in the same way the disciples walked with Jesus physically. We walk with him spiritually. He leads us through His word which shapes how we think about who He is, who we are and how we should respond to the trials we will encounter along the journey. Just as Jesus walked in real life with the disciples, Jesus walks in real life with us daily through the indwelling of His Spirit and the power of His Word. Jesus promised us His spirit to dwell in us to teach and lead us on our life's journey. He also gives us His Word to guide us in how to live on the journey. He has given us all we need to successfully complete this journey we call life and He will faithfully lead us step by step as we walk the journey together.

Let's start the journey by considering how suffering is impacting you today.

—————— Examining Our Trial/Suffering/Storm ——————

What is the current trial or struggle you are facing now?

Circle words that you can identify with as you face this struggle:

Anger	Numb	Seek Counsel
Fear	Harden	Avoid
Fixing	Self-Harm	Isolate
Control	Guilt	Self Hatred
Ignore	Shame	Hatred of Others
Escape	Work Harder	Other (list)
Medicate	Improve	

What desires do you have for this situation? (i.e., If this happened... or if I was... things would be better.)

What fears do you have about the situation?
(i.e., If I do/don't do this... this will happen.)

What words from the list can you identify with in this situation? What do you feel right now?

Hopeless	Unkind	Guilty
Lack of Peace	Quarrelsome	Regretful
Joyless	Lack of Gentleness	Peaceful
Anxious	Judgmental	Content
Stress	Condemning	Hopeful
Depression	Unforgiving	Life-Filled
Anger	Lonely	Joy
Discontentedness	Isolated	Self-Controlled
Lack of Self-Control	Misunderstood	Other (list)
Impatient	Shameful	

God is in the process of completing our spiritual growth journey through the everyday circumstances and relationships of our lives. And although our suffering may not be alleviated or resolved, we *can* live an abundant life full of peace, hope and joy. No matter what our current struggle is we are promised abundant life, unending hope, and everlasting joy. If that doesn't encompass your life now then know there is another way that leads to peace and joy and His name is Jesus.

Let's take a journey together with Jesus. It is a perilous journey with many winding paths, treacherous mountains and endless troubles. Just like the disciples, it will be the undoing of all that you are. If you're truly ready to live life fully, as God intended, be ready to toss your old navigation system as together we learn new ways to respond to our suffering as we journey with the One who calls "follow me."

CHAPTER ONE

THE STORY

God is telling His great story of salvation and redemption.
He desires to tell His story through our lives.

People love a good story. The story of life begins at conception and flows forward. Beginnings, endings, struggles, and triumphs—the plot lines of challenge, loss, and victory are woven into the reality of each person's story. The everyday happenings of people everywhere chronicle life, and no two tales are the same.

God has a story as well. His story originates outside of time, and its influence permeates the pages of history. His story, like all good stories, starts in the beginning.

God. Both author and central character.

He gave us the Bible so we may read and engage with His story. He knew we would need His words. For by His Word, all creation appeared, filled with amazing and dramatic displays of His holy power and creativity. The entire universe declares His glory.

How does God fit into your story?

The Glory of God

Glory is reflected in the physical creation that makes up our incredible world. But of all that God created, His masterpiece was man and woman. Adam and Eve were unlike the rest of God's incredible work; He crafted them with great love and care, in His own image. They reflected Him. He gave them incredible purpose—to bear His image, to be His worshippers. Fulfilling this mission required obedience, and lovingly serving and communing with the living God.

God created all to live in perfect harmony with Himself and with one another. The garden and the first moments of creation still sing a song of hope to the memories hidden within each soul. We wish to remember when Earth and all of creation were without decay, when all enjoyed tranquil peace with man and God. There was perfect love between God and His creation.

Tragically, one wrong decision covered Eden with despair. Disobedience entered into God's story. Adam and Eve were created in God's likeness, but they were not equal to God. God lovingly gave them rule over all of His creation and freedom to govern the whole earth, setting only one boundary—they were not to eat the fruit of one specific tree.

The Destruction of Man

Enter the antagonist. God's story had an enemy who desired to overthrow His rule. Satan presented God's image bearers with a new story, a tale that promised fictional satisfaction by replacing God as the central character. The villain promised Adam and Eve that they, too, could be like God. Satan, disguised as a serpent, lied to them and convinced them that God was not good and did not have their best interest in mind. Adam and Eve began to question the character of their creator and, in rebellion, chose to disobey God.

They feasted on the forbidden fruit, ushering sin into an innocent world. They chose to believe the Liar instead of the Living God. Adam and Eve determined that they could discern, apart from God, what was good. In doing so, what was evil became the center of *their* story. The image of God in man became distorted and marred by sin.

When you think about sin, what comes to mind?

In what ways have the consequences of sin affected your life?

Separation of God and Man

The consequences of Adam's and Eve's choice were horrific! Like an atomic bomb, sin entered into God's perfect story bringing with it the fallout of separation, destruction, and death. Sin's consequences brought a new reality into the created world— suffering and pain. All of creation was distorted from its original design. Now instead of peace and harmony, war, poverty, disease, greed, and scandals would plague humanity together with the rest of God's creation. Everything in God's perfect world was left broken.

God removed Adam and Eve from the garden as a result of their sinful choice to live outside of God's boundaries. But…God sent them away with a promise of rescue and hope! He told them of a seed (a baby). Their descendant would rescue all of mankind from sin. Throughout history, God continues to tell the story of His great love for His creation, separation because of sin, and His promise of salvation through a baby who would grow to make the ultimate and final payment for the sins of the whole world. God did not end His story after sin entered. Instead, He chose to continue it and reveal the greatest rescue plan ever carried out.

God's Salvation

The promised seed was simply God himself: a human baby named Jesus. The Bible records the fulfillment of all the Old Testament predictions God made about Jesus' birth, His life, and His death. Jesus lived a perfect and sinless life as He walked, taught, and lived among His own creation. He put on display, in human flesh, the living God of creation. But creation rejected His message and eventually cried out for His death, finally nailing Him to a cross.

What do you know/believe about Jesus?

This seemingly disastrous end to Jesus' ministry on Earth was the focal point of God's grand story. It was on the cross that Jesus took the penalty for every sin upon Himself. He bore sin for us so that we could have life in Him. This is the gift of salvation. Jesus accomplished this great salvation by willingly sacrificing Himself in our place. But the grave could not hold Him. Three days after He died on that cross, Jesus emerged from the tomb, fulfilling His earthly mission to defeat sin and death by rising from the dead, just as God had promised back in the garden.

God wants everyone to accept His great sacrifice, this salvation, as a means to restore our relationship with Him. Because it is sin that separates us from God, and Jesus' sacrifice in our place is the only way back to that relationship, we must believe in Christ for the forgiveness of sin. If we choose to reject Jesus' payment for our sin, then we choose eternal separation from the living God. This is literally Hell. This is why Jesus proclaims, "I am the way, and the truth, and the life. No one comes to the Father except through me." (John 14:6). Jesus now sits victorious at the right hand of His Father in Heaven where He reigns as the rightful King!

In what ways do you recognize your own need for salvation?

In what ways do you recognize Jesus as the
answer to your need for salvation?

Faith in Jesus Christ Alone

Faith is simple: trust in Jesus alone to save you. All of us have a sin issue that we are powerless to change on our own. Faith means that instead of believing we can rescue ourselves from sin, we exchange our unrighteousness for His righteousness, which was achieved by His death, burial and resurrection.

Faith in Jesus means that our allegiance is now to Him as the rightful King and ruler of our lives, and through His Spirit, we will be able to bow in humble obedience to His rule.

Jesus does not offer salvation as a promise that we will never suffer hardship on Earth, or that He will fulfill all our felt needs. Rather, He offers us the resolution to our deepest problem: sin. Once we are set free from our bondage to sin, we are then free to serve the living God and bear His image well as we journey through life. We are called to die to our own desires and now live for His. He is where we will find hope, joy, purpose, and meaning. He is where we find life (for more, see *Understanding My Salvation* on p. 22).

How does reading God's Story impact and change your story?

What will you do with God's story?

God's Great Story

God is telling His great story of salvation and redemption. He desires to tell His story through our lives. In submitting our life to His story, He again becomes the central character. He is the orchestrator and director, and His story's themes become the priority of our life's story.

Please share your story by answering these questions.

Write about situations or challenges you are currently facing.

Who are you able to talk to about your situation?

In what ways are you responding in this situation?

What relationships are affected? How are they affected?

How do you see God's hand at work in this
situation and where do you feel His silence?

UNDERSTANDING MY SALVATION

Justified

Justification is God's instantaneous and irreversible declaration that the unrighteous are made positionally righteous (Romans 3:24-28; 4:1-5; 5:1-2). We are forever wrapped in the everlasting righteousness of Christ! His record becomes our record. His merit becomes our merit. From the moment of salvation, God treats us as righteous. Like His Son, we become God's children (1 John 3:1).

Sanctified

Sanctification is a progressive process that spans the believer's life. The ongoing work of the Spirit conforms the believer to the image of Jesus (Romans 8:29). This process happens in the ordinary circumstances and relationships of our daily lives as we put into practice living in dependence and obedience to God through his Word, the Bible (Colossians 3:16), and by his Spirit (Psalm 143:10, Romans 8:14).

Glorified

Glorification is a future hope, an event in which the believer will be fully completed and perfected in Christ at the final Resurrection (Romans 5:2; Colossians 1:27). At that time, our bodies are made new, and we are permanently separated from sin and all of its consequences (2 Thessalonians 2:14; 2 Timothy 2:10). In light of this truth we can endure the brokenness of this current life, recognizing that our pain and suffering are light and momentary compared to the Glory that is to come (2 Corinthians 4:17-18).

I AM

CHAPTER TWO

WHO IS GOD?

Have you fashioned a god of your own making?

After trekking through ancient Aztec ruins in Mexico, a tourist discovered a little clay figure in one of the nearby shops enticing visitors. Frosted in dust, it clearly had sat long undisturbed on a back shelf. The shop owner quickly proclaimed this little clay god's importance. "You hold in your hands what many believed to be the great god and creator of the world."

A whole society was captivated by a belief in man-made gods carved out of rock or modeled in clay. This religious system of stone held no ability to actually fulfill what so many desperately believed in and hoped for. This clay god represented a spiritual structure now in ruins. Once worshipped, these dusty, dead gods are now pawned off for pennies in tourist shops.

It is easy to identify that this little clay god was man's attempt to appeal to some higher power for help and resources, but can we also recognize our own tendency to create *a god in our own image*? A tangible, relatable and accessible god who looks and acts like us?

Circle the terms you would choose to describe how you see God:

Controlling	Condemning	Whimsical
Loving	Concerned	Authoritative
Distant	Angry	Benevolent
Kind	Unloving	Sovereign
Absent	Shepherding	Powerful
Judgmental	Impotent	

Who is God, Really?

How we view God is very important. The Bible declares that a false view of God or a *god of our own making* is idolatry (Isaiah 44:9-20; Leviticus 19:4). We tend to define God in human terms that relate more closely to how we think and act than to who He truly is. God shows us this truth when He says, "You thought that I was one like yourself" (Psalm 50:21). We attribute human qualities to God when we make him appear to look and act more like fallen humanity than the perfect, righteous and holy God of the Bible.

Consider some of the following human descriptions of God. Have you ever thought of God in these ways? Circle those points you relate to.

- *God is like my father:* Our experience with our earthly father, good or bad, often influences how we view God.
- *God is like a vending machine:* When we deposit our good deeds, actions and prayers, we expect an appropriate payout of what we believe will meet our current need.
- *God is like a clock maker:* He created and wound the clock just to let it run its course. He is uninvolved and disconnected with the unfolding of the human story being lived out in this world.

- *God is like a cosmic cop:* He is waiting for the moment we step out of His boundaries to bring down judgment and punishment. He's legalistic, authoritative, and doles out pain and suffering as consequences for disobedience.
- *God is like a best friend:* He desires to help us find our best life now. He has no expectations of us but exists to ensure we have whatever we believe will fulfill us. If we see God as someone who really doesn't care how we live, then our actions don't matter at all. We reduce Him to a good old drinking buddy, who doesn't really want what is best for us or care to challenge us to live for Christ – rather He just wants us to "feel" good about who we are and what we do.

Are there other human qualities you might be attributing to God?

Once God is redefined on our own terms, we are susceptible to worshipping whatever our heart desires. We are worshipful beings. We will either worship a holy and righteous God or creation itself (Romans 1:18-32). What our hearts most desire will become our god. What we desire or fear will dictate what we live for.

Why Do We Worship a God of Our Own Making?

There are many reasons; consider each of these three areas:

1. We don't know God because we haven't studied His Word, the Bible.

The world (which is ruled by Satan) is continually attacking/ suppressing the true knowledge of God and presenting false saviors (idols) to worship (i.e. money, power, sex). If we are not consistently going back to the Bible to remind ourselves who God says He is, then we will easily be influenced by who we, the world, our circumstances and/or our relationships say God is.

Do you want to know God? What are you doing to find out more about who He is?

2. We feel overwhelmed by trials and suffering.

A young woman, who had experienced a life of trauma and abuse as a child, could easily describe the God of the Bible as loving, powerful, creator, sovereign. But when pressed to describe God as she personally experienced Him, she used very different terms. She described herself being a broken, bleeding child lying on the ground while God stood over her, looking down at her but choosing to do nothing to help or comfort her. She concluded that God was able because she had been taught in church about his power and his abilities to help and to love and to protect. She also concluded that either God is truly evil or she was so ugly and defiled that even God ignored her in her desperation and need.

When life is painful, chaotic and out of control, we begin to define God by our experience and/or feelings. It is easy to equate the character and nature of God with what we experience in our lives. If we have had a difficult, destructive, abusive experience where it seemed God was distant, uncaring or cruel, it is easy to let the suffering begin to define God instead of knowing and choosing to believe who He has proclaimed Himself to be in His Word.

In what ways have trials and suffering influenced how you view God?

3. We want to take charge of our own lives.

It is easy to miss one of the biggest challenges in seeing and knowing God accurately: self. Self-orientation, in other words, thinking more highly of self than God, usurps the rightful rule of God in our hearts. We elevate our own wisdom, or the wisdom and philosophies of man over the truth proclaimed in the Bible. Just like we breathe without giving it a second thought, we live continually loving self, serving self, protecting self, promoting self. It is natural and automatic. We will find ourselves continually suppressing the truth of who God is in order to live out what comes naturally to us, a self-ruled heart.

What does your heart desire most?
Circle any words you can identify with:

Money	Comfort	Success
Power	Escape	Rest
Love	Adventure	Health
Security	Consistency	Control
Reputation	Sex	Write in your own:

Seeing God Accurately

We see the evidence of God and His goodness all around us: in the marvels of the created world and the existence and complexities of the universe, in the intricate details of our amazing bodies, and in the moral code imbedded in us, individually and collectively, as beings created in God's image. We see the masterful, overwhelming fingerprints of God everywhere we look—if we have eyes to see.

The Bible puts language to the character, nature, and glory of God. It tells about His righteousness, His mercy, His justice and His love. The Bible exalts Him above all. God's greatest desire is that the entire world would see, know and love Him. God sent His Son in human form, Jesus, as a living expression of God's love for us. Is truth instructing and informing your thinking about who He is or have you created a god of your own making? *A right view of God will bring rest, peace and joy in a broken, fallen world.* Let's look in His Word and see what He declares about Himself. Take time to read the verses listed for each one.

Who is God? – His Nature

- God is spirit, by nature intangible (John 4:24)
- God is One, but He exists as three Persons—God the Father, God the Son, and God the Holy Spirit (Matthew 3:16-17)
- God is without boundaries, King of the ages, immortal, invisible, only God (1 Timothy 1:17)
- God is incomparable (2 Samuel 7:22)
- God is unchanging (Malachi 3:6)
- God exists everywhere (Psalm 139:7-12)
- God knows everything (Psalm 147:5; Isaiah 40:28)
- God has all power and authority (Revelation 19:6)

Who is God? – His Character

- God is just (Acts 17:31)
- God is loving (Ephesians 2:4-5)
- God is truthful (John 14:6)
- God is holy (1 John 1:5).
- God shows compassion (2 Corinthians 1:3)
- God shows mercy (Romans 9:15)
- God gives grace (Romans 5:17)
- God judges sin (Psalm 5:5)
- God offers forgiveness (Psalm 130:4; 1 John1:9)

Who is God? – His Actions

- God created the world (Genesis 1:1; Isaiah 42:5)
- God actively sustains the world (Colossians 1:17)
- God is executing His eternal plan (Ephesians 1:11) which involves rescuing man from the curse of sin and death (Galatians 3:13-14)
- God draws people to Christ (John 6:44)
- God disciplines His children (Hebrews 12:6)
- God will judge the world (Revelation 20:11-15)
- God is with us, Emmanuel (Mathew 1:23)

God has always desired to be with and to dwell with His creation. He created us to find our ultimate fulfillment in Him by loving Him, depending on Him, and obeying Him. This was all made possible by giving His Son. God in human form, Jesus, was born into the world He created. So, to really know who God is, all we have to do is look at Jesus!

Which of these (God's nature, character, and actions) do you struggle to believe in your current circumstances?

So, What About You?

While awaiting his execution in prison, Paul wrote these words, "Which is why I suffer as I do. But I am not ashamed, *for I know whom I have believed, and I am convinced that he is able to guard until that day what has been entrusted to me*"–2 Timothy 1:12. Paul did not define God through his circumstances or relationships. Instead Paul took God at His Word and believed who God revealed Himself to be. This intimate knowledge of God shaped everything in Paul's life, even his suffering and his death.

What Paul believed about God produced rest, peace and joy, in spite of the horrific circumstances that Paul experienced in his life (beatings, imprisonment, prejudice to name a few). A right view of God will always produce internal rest, peace and joy regardless of how difficult or overwhelming our current circumstances or relationships seem. Therefore, if we continually struggle to find rest, peace and/or joy internally, then we should investigate whether or not we are viewing God accurately.

Choosing to see God through a biblical lens will greatly impact how you experience, interpret, and respond to your circumstances and relationships. *We must always investigate which lens through which we are choosing to view God and our trials.*

A BIBLICAL VIEW OF GOD

GOD IS

Perfect in Love

God demonstrates His love for us in that while we were still sinners, He gave His life for us (Romans 5:8). His sacrificial death on the cross as payment for our sins is the ultimate expression of love. In keeping with His nature, *He only does what is most loving for us* (Romans 8:37-39, 1 John 4 :9-11).

Infinite in Wisdom

God's wisdom is beyond our understanding. God doesn't just know and understand all things, He is the ultimate source of all wisdom and knowledge (Psalms 147:5, Romans 11:33). The Bible says that His thoughts are beyond our thoughts and that His ways are not our ways (Isaiah 55:8-9). In keeping with His nature *He always knows what is best for us.*

Completely Sovereign

God is the supreme authority and all things are under His control (Colossians 1:16). He will bring about what is most loving and *what He knows is best for us.*

Reflection/Journal

CHAPTER THREE

WHO IS MAN?

Our circumstances and relationships become the
context God uses to put our heart on display, to show us
whom our heart is oriented to, whether God or self.

As a kid, Josh took a skills course in orienteering. He remembered learning how to use a compass and being amazed at how it worked. He grew to trust it. No matter how turned around he was, he could find his way through uncharted territory with the aid of his compass. It was reliable and steadfast; it never changed. It was anchored to true north. He never feared getting lost as long as he carried it.

One day, he and his friends decided to trek into uncharted wilderness, beyond their typical boundaries of adventuring. They journeyed, explored, and tested their bravery as they experienced new and undiscovered places. At some point, they realized Josh had dropped his compass. Suddenly, the trees seemed larger, the sounds more savage, and the forest more foreboding. The wildness of the world becomes much more daunting when you have no guide.

They backtracked for a while and drew a breath of relief when one of them discovered the compass amid the rocky terrain. As delighted as Josh was to find it, he was alarmed to also find that it was broken. The trusty arrow that previously anchored his direction, now aimlessly spun in circles. It no longer showed true north and, therefore had lost its intended purpose. They abandoned his compass and had to rely on their own sense of direction to get them home.

Running low on supplies and physically exhausted, hope in their ability to rescue themselves out of their circumstances waned. Their ability to find their own way without a compass was more than just hindered—it was devastatingly crippled.

They learned a valuable lesson—one that served to bring insight and grounding in consequent years.

Our own lives are like that damaged compass. Because of sin, we are broken and lost. We have no capacity to go the right direction.

A broken compass will always lead us off course. But there is One who is able to guide and direct our path through the difficult terrain of this life. There is One we can depend on who will never break, forsake, or lead astray, and that One is Jesus. He is not merely anchored to north—He *is* true north. He alone can lead us home.

Until we realize and admit our own brokenness and inability to lead ourselves through the difficult terrain of life, we remain lost. In recognizing our brokenness, we can—indeed we must—continually orient our lives to the Living God, who is our true north.

Our Internal Compass

Just as a broken compass is useless to provide guidance and direction, so is our own internal compass—our heart. Once anchored to true north, since our fall we remain hopelessly damaged by sin. Our internal navigational center—our heart—

now aimlessly wanders. We naturally orient our hearts to our own desires instead of to the Living God. This ultimately leads to destruction. In our brokenness, we abandon true north and depend instead on self-orientation, our own senses and experiences, to navigate through life. Our heart gravitates toward relationships and circumstances, hoping for fulfillment, purpose and ultimately "life."

As you consider your current circumstances and relationships, reflect on these Self-Oriented statements from the book of Proverbs. Do any of these actions reflect your current thinking and feelings? They are good indicators of being self-oriented/self-ruled instead of God-oriented or Christ-Ruled.

Evidence from Proverbs of a Life that is Self-Ruled:

- Is convinced he is right (12:15)
- Quickly shows his annoyance (12:16)
- Is hotheaded and reckless (14:16)
- Spurns discipline and correction (15:5)
- Wastes money (17:16)
- Delights in airing his own opinions (18:2)
- Is quick to quarrel (20:3)
- Scorns wisdom (23:9)
- Is wise in his own eyes (26:5)
- Trusts in himself (28:26)
- Rages and scoffs, and there is no peace around him (29:9)

Consider which of the previous statements from Scripture describe you. In your own words, describe how this looks in your life.

Our Heart

When we come to salvation through the gracious gift of God's son Jesus Christ (by faith, Ephesians 2:8-9), we are made new (2 Corinthians 5:17) and given a new heart (Ezekiel 11:19). Now a greater force than self-rule fills our heart: The Holy Spirit of God (1 Corinthians 6:19). If we live in obedience to and dependence on the Holy Spirit then He will produce the fruits of His Spirit as stated in Scripture. Letting the Word of God dwell in you (Colossians 3:16) and the Holy Spirit guide, convict and instruct you moment-by-moment, will produce the fruit of the Spirit.

Consider the following verse.
Would this verse describe you generally?

"But the fruit of the Spirit is love, joy, peace, patience, kindness, goodness, faithfulness, gentleness, self-control; against such things there is no law." (Galatians 5:22-23)

If this verse isn't representative of your life, why not?
What hinders the Spirit's work through you?

Our Choice

Upon salvation we make a choice about who rules our heart—our self (our own internal compass) or the Holy Spirit (a Christ-ruled heart). We can choose to place Christ on the throne of our heart by living in obedience to and dependence on the Spirit and His Word.

We think we are wise and full of understanding, but, in reality, our own sinful hearts deceive us. Just as that broken compass would lack the ability to provide accurate guidance and lead us to a specific destination, so too our self-ruled heart will never lead us to "truth". We inevitably lead ourselves on paths to fulfill our own sinful desires—aimlessly wandering, unanchored, lost, and without hope or direction. We do not see our own heart or our internal compass accurately. We are deceived.

The heart is command central for our thoughts, feelings and actions. ***Whoever rules the heart rules the life.*** The only options for ruling are:

- God, through His son Jesus Christ (Christ-rule)
- Self through our own deceitful and wicked heart (self-rule)

The rule and purposes of our heart are the most powerful and significant forces in our thinking, feelings and actions. Our heart determines what, why and how we do what we do. ***The course we follow in our lives is determined by who rules the heart.*** Consider how Jesus describes our internal compass in Luke 6:43-45:

"For no good tree bears bad fruit, nor again does a bad tree bear good fruit, for each tree is known by its own fruit. For figs are not gathered from thornbushes, nor are grapes picked from a bramble bush. The good person [Christ-ruled] out of the good treasure of his heart produces good [Christ-like characteristics, the fruit of the Spirit], and the evil person [self-ruled] out of his evil treasure produces evil [fleshly fruit], for out of the abundance of the heart his mouth speaks."

Consider examples of both the fruit of the Spirit and fleshly fruit in your own life.

Jesus compares the truths we find in the created world. Good, healthy trees produce good, healthy fruit. Likewise bad, or unhealthy trees produce bad or unhealthy fruit. The fruit's quality is external evidence of the tree's internal health, or lack thereof.

So it is with our heart. If our life mirrors the list from Proverbs, our heart is self-ruled. On the other hand, Christ-like fruit (love, joy, peace, patience, kindness, goodness, faithfulness, gentleness, self-control –Galatians 5:22-23a) indicates a Christ-ruled heart.

This passage in Luke helps us to understand ourselves and why we behave the way we do. Whoever rules our heart (Christ or self), rules our life and the evidence of who rules is seen in the fruit that is produced in our life (fleshly or Christ-like).

Our Heart is Deceived

We do not see our heart the way God sees it. Our heart's lustful desire is oriented to ourselves (self-rule). We will crown ourselves as ruler and reign over our own self-made kingdom (self-oriented). In Jeremiah 17:9, God describes our internal compass—which is broken and self-ruled—this way:

"The heart is deceitful above all things, and desperately wicked; Who can know it?" (NKJV)

So who is the first person our heart deceives? Ourselves, of course. Our own heart deceives us. Our heart buys the lies that Satan sells, telling us that "life" can be grasped by controlling our circumstances and relationships. Circumstances and relationships, like magnets, draw our deceived and unanchored heart away from truth.

Do you recognize areas of your heart that are deceitful or desperately wicked?

Our Heart is Wicked

In Jeremiah, the word **wicked** is preceded by the descriptive word desperately, emphasizing the extreme degree of the heart's wickedness. Righteousness, goodness and love are unattainable from within ourselves. Our best actions of love and justice are but filthy rags (Isaiah 64:6) when motivated by the desires of our deceitful and wicked heart.

Self-ruled expressions of love for the relationships in our lives are always first and foremost self-oriented and self-seeking. We use manipulation, guilt, intimidation, or coercion to control our circumstances, to achieve fulfillment. If only our savings account were bigger; if only my spouse would get counseling; if only I got this specific degree, or promotion; if only I were able to get pregnant, then my life would be... fulfilled, safe, predictable, comfortable. We love with condition and expectation. We orchestrate with manipulation and coercion. We seek to control the relationships and the circumstances in our lives to bring us "life."

What "if only" statements are you making in your own life?

Who Knows My Heart?

God wants us to understand our own sinfulness and brokenness. Let's consider Jeremiah's final statement about our heart, "who can know it"? Do you think you know your heart? According to God you do not! God says He is the only one who truly sees our heart accurately. Because God does know our heart and the depth of our brokenness, He is dedicated to exposing our sin. He faithfully uses our circumstances and relationships to reveal what He already knows. *Our circumstances and relationships become the context God uses to put our heart on display, to show us whom our heart is oriented to, whether God or self.*

What have your current circumstances revealed about your heart's orientation?

Recognize, Repent, Replace

Like magnets that pull a compass arrow away from true north, so too are our circumstances and relationships. If we don't surrender to Christ's rule in our lives, the things in our lives with the strongest gravitational pull will set our course and our direction. Career, education, financial security, spouse, children, parents, or friends can operate like magnets. Therefore, we must learn to recognize our own heart's deceitful promise of finding fulfillment in these areas. We must learn to continually correct course, so our thinking, feeling and actions line up with God's truth. God desires that we would continually examine our lives for evidence of self-rule, or navigating through life with a broken compass. When God graciously reveals our heart through our circumstances and relationships, we can quickly *recognize* our self-rule, *repent* of our sin and *replace* Christ as our rightful ruler. God graciously forgives and will re-orient our heart to His own.

RECOGNIZE-REPENT-REPLACE

RECOGNIZE ○ My thoughts and actions.
What do I need to "put off?"

"Let all bitterness and wrath and anger and clamor and slander be put away from you, along with all malice." –Ephesians 4:31

"But now you must put them all away: anger, wrath, malice, slander, and obscene talk from your mouth. Do not lie to one another, seeing that you have put off the old self with its practices." –Colossians 3:8-9

REPENT ○ Confess my sin, turn and walk in a new direction.
To change one's mind, walking away from
sin and towards God.

"If we confess our sins, he is faithful and just to forgive us our sins and to cleanse us from all unrighteousness." –1 John 1:9

REPLACE ○ God's thoughts and actions.
What do I need to "put on?"

"Put on then, as God's chosen ones, holy and beloved, compassionate hearts, kindness, humility, meekness, and patience, bearing with one another and, if one has a complaint against another, forgiving each other; as the Lord has forgiven you, so you also must forgive. And above all these put on love, which binds everything together in perfect harmony." –Colossians 3:12-14

CHAPTER FOUR

WHOSE KINGDOM?

Who rules your heart will determine whose kingdom you live in.

While touring antique shops on the East Coast, an Englishman visiting the US for seminary training came across an old poster from the Revolutionary War. He was stunned and deeply concerned by what he read. "We will serve no sovereign here!" the poster proclaimed. His heart sank for a people who, in fierce self-determination, would have no King rule over their lives. What he acknowledged as a political and revolutionary statement, he also recognized as a spiritual defect in the heart of every man and woman who rebels against the rule of God, our true King. We often likewise reject the sovereign reign of the living God and place ourselves on the throne of our own kingdoms.

When we reject God as King, we boldly crown our "self" as reigning sovereign. Though we may not recognize our own self-rule, it becomes evident in our responses to circumstances and relationships in our lives, for "out of our hearts our mouths speak" (Luke 6:45). If our heart rules (self-rule) it will produce external evidence of the flesh (Galatians 5:19-20). If Christ rules, we will live in obedience to and dependence on the Spirit and will produce the Fruit of the Spirit (Galatians 5:22-25). This evidence is how we can recognize who is ruling our hearts. ***Who rules our heart will determine whose kingdom we live in.***

Evidence of the flesh

A heart in rebellion against God's reign and kingdom expresses itself in opposition to what God says it looks like to live in His kingdom. God's Word says that the products of a self-ruled heart are easy to recognize.

Consider and underline what you recognize in your own life from this paraphrase of Galatians 5:19-20:

A self-ruled heart generates wrong desires about sex and wrong ways of thinking about and using sex. It worships and desires God's creation (people and things) instead of God Himself. It produces hatred towards others, it argues, it is jealous, it is angry, it is self-centered. It produces opposition between people, divisions in relationship, and is drawn to false teachers. It is envious. It chases after opportunities to indulge in fleeting (and often destructive) pleasures—getting drunk, getting high and expressing hearty approval of others who do likewise.

God's Word says that these behaviors are not part of His kingdom. Therefore, if they *are* part of our lives, then we are clearly not living under His rule or in His kingdom but are rather crowning our own heart and its sinful desires. If these behaviors characterize our lives, it is possible we have never accepted His invitation to be a part of His kingdom. We still live in the domain of darkness (our own sinful self-ruled heart) and are not yet transferred to the kingdom of His beloved son (Colossians 1:13).

Have you received God's free gift? His Son lived a perfect life, died on the cross to pay for all sin, and rose again on the third day, demonstrating His power over sin and death. This is salvation, which once received, transfers us from the darkness of our sinful world into God's kingdom, where He rules in our hearts and lives (John 3:16, 1 Corinthians 15:1-4, Acts 16:31).

Reflect on evidence of the flesh in your life:

Because of our deceitful and wicked heart, we are born committed to our own self-rule and our own kingdom. We are naturally hostile to all other kingdoms but our own, especially the kingdom of the living God. Part of accepting His gift of salvation is accepting His rule and reign. We must continue to humble ourselves and live in obedience to and dependence on Him.

Our own self-rule is often the reason why we suppress the

truth about who God is (Romans 1:18-20). We do not want to serve a sovereign God because we must then subjugate our self-rule to Him. So we create a god of our own making to ensure the survival of our own kingdom. We choose open rebellion against our Sovereign and proclaim with fierce determination in our hearts, "I will serve no sovereign here!"

God's Kingdom

When we turn to Jesus Christ for our salvation, He places us in His Kingdom—a spiritual kingdom. Similar to our physical birth into a family, we are spiritually born into God's family and God's Kingdom with all the rights, resources, and privileges of a son or daughter of the King. We can do nothing to gain entrance into the Kingdom; we cannot earn, work or force our way in. Our entrance is a personal invitation by the King Himself to be His heir and child. We accept this invitation by faith—trusting Him to save us. Once we are placed in the Kingdom, we do not have to work to keep our status. We are His children and citizens of His kingdom because of this gracious and merciful gift.

Ways We Try to Gain God's Acceptance or Approval:

- Spending time in God's Word (and how often)
- Scripture Memorization
- Church Attendance
- Prayer
- Being the Perfect Wife, Husband, Dad, Mom, Friend, Servant, Worker, Student
- Staying away from certain "sins" or "gray areas"

What behaviors do you believe you have to perform to keep yourself saved?

God gives us His Word to guide us. It shows us how to thrive in His Kingdom. Though keeping His laws doesn't save us, they are in place to protect and prosper His citizens through good and difficult times. God is always good, righteous, and just—a King who is motivated by His love, His infinite wisdom, and His sovereign control.

In His Kingdom there is no judgment or condemnation. We are free from fear of punishment because Jesus paid the just penalty for our self-rule and replaces it with His righteousness that He provides to each heir to His Kingdom.

Describe how you think God responds to you when you have sinned or gotten off track:

Motivated By Love

As ones who have experienced His grace and mercy, we are called to humbly live in dependence and obedience to His rule and reign. We are also called to choose to make His law the desire of our hearts and live in submission to His dictates. In His Kingdom, we have life (John 10:10, John 14:6).

Because we understand the great cost Jesus paid at the cross to redeem us to Himself and place us in His kingdom, we are motivated by His love to submit to His kingdom rule, and to live life for His glory.

How does God's love motivate you?

Kingdom Conflict

When we repress and reject the living God for a god of our own making, we also reject the Kingdom that He rules and invites us to live in. While we, through salvation, can live spiritually in

God's Kingdom, we often find ourselves living in open rebellion to our sovereign King, and instead, we live, for all practical purposes, in a kingdom of our own. With our puppet king and our kingdom in place, we borrow Christian language, religious activities, and moral behaviors to legitimize our own self-rule. We deceive ourselves into believing we worship and live for Him, while, in reality, we fulfill our own desires. Fears and ungodly desires and our own prosperity become our motivation. We place a big religious stamp of approval on our own actions, while we live in continual opposition to the true King and Kingdom for which we were rescued. We exchange the glory of God for the broken mortal glory of man, and destroy ourselves in the process.

The Self-Ruled Kingdom

When we sit on the throne of our own lives, we become the:

- *Law-maker*
- *Judge*
- *Dispenser of punishment/reward*

Unlike the righteous King who reigns in justice and love, we are unjust, unloving, and ruled by our own deceived and wicked heart (Jeremiah 17:9). Everyone in our lives becomes a pawn in our kingdom, manipulated for our own gain and personal fulfillment. We expect others, ourselves, and even our God to meet our expectations: If my husband really cared about my feelings, he would not ask me to have sex with him so often; If I was a good parent, my children would behave better; If God really loved me, He would not have allowed this to happen to me.

What are some of your expectations of God,
self and others in your kingdom?

God:

Self:

Others:

When our expectations are unfulfilled, we judge others, ourselves, and our god. As our own sovereign, we alone have the right to hold court and sit as judge to determine how God, self and others have lived up to our expectations (laws).

In what ways do you judge God, self, others?
Describe how this looks in your life.

God:

Self:

Others:

Once we judge that our expectations have not been met, we dispense our punishment (verbal assault, guilt, physical punishment, withholding of relationship, intimidation, threats, self-harm) or reward accordingly. Everything must conform to our self-ruled desires in order to ensure ultimate compliance and our kingdom's continuing reign and prosperity.

In what ways do you dispense punishment
or reward to God, self and others?

God:

Self:

Others:

How do we rationalize our self-ruled kingdom? Are we trying
to save ourselves through our good works? (see Galatians 3:2-3)
Are we trying to grow in our faith by our flesh, our own human
efforts to please God? Whose righteousness are we appealing to,
God's or our own? These are good questions to ask as we look
more closely at whose kingdom are we living in.

Consider some common answers to these questions. Which ones sound familiar (which are most similar to your own methods)?

- By religious efforts—moral law-keeping (being a good person).
- By irreligious efforts—personal law-keeping (living according to my own expectations and self-made laws).
- By innate goodness or purity—something in me is good and right (I am basically a good person).
- By abstaining from really bad behavior—keeping a short or mild sin list (not an addict, prostitute, murderer or thief).
- By emotional stability—feeling good, clean and in control of circumstances and relationships.[1]

How do you believe you gain entrance into God's kingdom and grow spiritually?

[1] Taken from *Equipped to Counsel* by John Henderson, Second Edition, p. 139.

The feelings and behaviors produced by our thought patterns demonstrate whose kingdom we are truly serving.

Consider the following and circle any that describe your perspective.*

- I feel entitled to pleasant circumstances from God when I've done what pleases Him.
- I feel bitter or angry when God does not meet my expectations, in my way and on my schedule.
- I feel impatient toward others' mistakes or lack of meeting my expectations.
- I feel frantic to keep rules and expectations.
- I feel longstanding guilt and shame over my failures.
- I feel that God is a frowning, quick-tempered and/or aloof Judge.
- I feel that God is out to get me or arbitrarily brings bad things into my life.[2]

These feelings and thought patterns indicate that we rule our own kingdom. They result from our wrong view of God and what it means to live in His kingdom.

God orchestrates our circumstances and relationships to reveal who rules our heart. This is His grace gift to us. The ability to see what God reveals and to recognize our blind spots (remember, our hearts are deceitful) is His continued demonstration of love toward us. Lean into His blessing by *recognizing* how our deceitful and wicked hearts rule. Once recognized we can quickly *repent* of our sinful self-rule and *invite* God back onto His throne and allow Him to rightly rule over our lives.

[2] Taken from *Equipped to Counsel* by John Henderson, Second Edition, p. 139.

God's Kingdom Blessings

Though we often presume God's condemnation, judgment, or anger toward us, this is not an accurate description of our King. He holds no wrath in His heart toward those whom He saves. He only desires our repentance so we may experience once again His gracious favor and right relationship.

In God's Kingdom, we are free from the fear of punishment. While God *disciplines* those whom He loves (Hebrews 12:5-7), only those who reject His free gift of salvation, His invitation to citizenship, and Kingdom inheritance need fear His *punishment*. He will judge sin righteously (Romans 6:23). However, His children, whose sins are forgiven and have received His gift of grace, have nothing to fear.

The Solution

Now consider the benefits of living under the rule and reign of God and His Kingdom. We are citizens and heirs because of His gift to us—the gift of faith that enables us to receive the resources and blessings of being His child. We no longer keep His Law—a standard of perfection impossible for mere humans to reach—to gain His approval; we are under grace!

In what ways does the offer and reality of freedom from meeting expectations, from condemnation and punishment impact your current circumstances?

WHO DOES GOD SAY I AM?

I AM —

Forgiven (Psalm 32:1)

Redeemed (Galatians 3:13-14)

Rescued (Colossians 1:13-14)

Healed (Psalm 107:19-21)

Set Free (Galatians 5:1)

Chosen (1 Peter 2:9-10)

Sealed (Ephesians 1:13)

Sanctified (Hebrews 10:14)

Protected (2 Thessalonians 3:3)

Created in His Image (Genesis 1:27)

Transformed (2 Corinthians 3:18)

Rooted and Established (Colossians 2:6-7)

Adopted (Ephesians 1:5)

Fearfully and Wonderfully Made (Psalm 139:13-16)

His Ambassador (2 Corinthians 5:20)

Loved (1 John 4:10)

Taught, Reproved, Corrected and Trained (2 Timothy 3:16)

Disciplined (Hebrews 12:5-11)

Lavished With Grace (Ephesians 1:7-9)

Growing (2 Peter 3:18)

How do these truths impact how you think and respond to your current life circumstances in His Kingdom?

If we do not see the living God accurately, we will inevitably create for ourselves gods of our own making and kingdoms of our own creation. We will live in continual bondage to our own self-rule and for the survival of our created domain. In the Bible, God gives us the means by which we can demolish the destructive tendency of our own desire to self-rule. Jesus clearly states that if we want to follow Him, we must deny ourselves (Luke 9:23). God understood how deeply influenced we are by our heart even after salvation and how we would need to continually choose to deny our own strong tendency to self-rule in our lives. This is only possible when we accurately see and continually seek God through His Word and in association with other Jesus-followers. By continually giving Him the honor and respect due Him, and seeing Him for who He is, we will know true and lasting joy. When we choose to submit our will and desires to His rule we can live in dependent obedience in His joy-filled Kingdom.

WHOSE KINGDOM?

SELF-RULED

You Become the Lawmaker

"Having begun by the Spirit,
are you now being
perfected by the flesh?..."
–Galatians 3:1-5

You Make Yourself Judge

"Judge not, that you be
not judged. For with the
judgment you pronounce
you will be judged..."
–Matthew 7:1-5

You Dispense Punishment

"Behold, blessed is the
one whom God reproves;
therefore despise not the
discipline of the Almighty."
–Job 5:17

BONDAGE

"Then desire when it has conceived
gives birth to sin, and sin when it is
fully grown brings forth death."
–James 1:15

CHRIST-RULED

Not Under the Law

"For by grace you
have been saved..."
–Ephesians 2:8

Not Under Judgment
or Condemnation

"There is therefore now
no condemnation..."
–Romans 8:1

Not Deserving of
Punishment and Death

"For the wages of sin is death,
but the free gift of God
is eternal life..."
–Romans 6:23

FREEDOM

"So if the Son sets you free,
you will be free indeed."
–John 8:36

CHAPTER FIVE

WHO RULES?

Who rules your heart determines who rules your life.

Brian and Amy attended high school youth group at the same church and started dating in college. They shared a lot in common. Both came from the same town, grew up in the same community of believers, and maintained a good testimony during their teen years.

Brian had high expectations of life. Success came easily. His home life had been fairly smooth, and he maintained healthy relationships with his parents and family. Brian believed hard work, faith, and family would ensure continued success into the future. Amy's life experiences, while similar, were more turbulent behind the scenes. Amy's father had been a strict disciplinarian. As an influential member of the community and the church, he desired to protect and preserve his reputation. Because of his need for community approval, he required complete submission from his wife and children. He controlled their home with an iron fist, using fear and intimidation to keep everyone in line. Amy saw her mother's hopes and dreams crushed beneath her father's overblown need for respect. Amy vowed never to allow anyone to rule her life the way her father had.

When Brian and Amy married, it seemed like a match made in Heaven. They had all the makings of a great marriage. Or so they (and everyone else) thought. Five years and two children later, their marriage was at a breaking point. They had not only fallen out of love, they had come to hate and despise each other. Brian and Amy desired to love God and love each other but were each ruled by their own hearts; driven by a variety of fears and desires.

Only a heart ruled by Christ will produce both the peace and contentment that will free Amy and Brian—and us—to love God, others, and each other.

Through Jesus' triumph on the cross over sin, we are set free from our enslavement to sin and self-rule, and freed to choose dependent obedience to Christ in our lives. With a Christ-ruled heart, we experience His gifts of peace and joy as we humbly submit to His Word and to the Holy Spirit. Loving and serving God and others is the natural outflow of a Christ-ruled heart.

The alternative is self-ruled indulgence in our own sinful nature. We serve and love ourselves, driven by our own desires and fears. Notice how we choose not just to love or to not love, rather we choose to love God or to love ourselves. Every moment we choose whom we will serve: God or self.

Identifying the ruler of our heart is the key to change and growth. Only a heart fully surrendered to the Eternal King can love God and others in a way that glorifies God and reflects His image in us. Look at the *"Who Rules Your Heart—Self-Ruled"* chart (pp. 80-81). Then continue reading the story about Brian and Amy. Look for ways your story might fit the same model.

Brian and Amy likely did not recognize that their self-ruled hearts came into their marriage with them. They gave lip service to their love for each other and their love for God, but in reality, they were most "in love" with themselves. Brian's desire to continue on the easy path of success in life and in relationships seemed attainable to him only if Amy and the kids fell in line with his plan. But every time Brian presented his plan to move his marriage, career, and/or family in that direction, Amy instinctively felt his effort to control. In fear she shut down and shut him out, thereby expressing her own need to control the circumstance and relationships in her life. The constant battle between Brian's desire for a fulfilled life and Amy's fear of Brian's control threatened to destroy their marriage.

Setting the Stage

Our growth and maturity depend on our ability to identify who rules our heart. How we react to people and experiences becomes the stage upon which the drama of "Who Rules" is acted out. We use circumstances and relationships in our lives to obtain our desires or to protect us from what we fear. God uses our circumstances and relationships to reveal what our heart worships, giving us the opportunity to recognize, repent of our self-rule and replace Christ back on the throne. Under His reign, we are free from the bondage of desire and fear, and we instead experience the blessings of peace and joy.

Exposing Our Heart

Hebrews 4:12 says that the Word of God is able to expose the "thoughts and intentions of the heart." This is God's desire—that in the middle of circumstances and relationships, our hearts (and who rules us) would be revealed. He also desires that we would examine what is being produced out of our innermost being and be cleansed from all unrighteousness. "For out of the abundance of the heart the mouth speaks." (Luke 6:45).

Who rules your heart determines who rules your life.

What do you think about the previous statement?

A Self-Ruled Heart

Desires and Fears

A prideful, self-ruled heart is plagued by either desire or fear. A self-centered heart desires what it does not have or is anxious and fears losing what it believes it needs. Like a two-sided coin, engraved on one side is "desire" and on the other is "fear". If I desire money, then I will also fear the loss of it, or if I desire human approval, I will equally fear disapproval.

In the book of Hebrews God explains, "Keep your life free from love of money, and be content with what you have, for he has said, 'I will never leave you nor forsake you.' So we can confidently say, 'The Lord is my helper; I will not fear; What can man do to me?'" –Hebrews 13:5-6

Notice how God places "love of money" (desire) in direct relationship to "being afraid" (fear). We desire what we believe will provide for or fulfill us, and we fear what threatens to take it away. When we fear what others will do to us, then we desire what we think will make us safe and secure.[1]

The answer to our self-rule is also presented in the passage. It is Jesus, the Lord of Lords. He alone is the fulfillment of our deepest desire, and relief from our greatest fear. He offers His own care and provision so we need not live in bondage to desire and fear.

Reflection/Journal

---

[1] Paraphrased from *Equipped to Counsel* by John Henderson, Second Edition, p. 178.

Consider the following groupings of desires and fears and circle the ones that best reflect your own.

Desire

Approval
Acceptance
Success
Money
Sexual Pleasure
Honor
Emotional Pleasure
Entertainment
Marriage
Children
A Good Marriage
Good Children
Possessions
Fulfillment
Health
Cleanliness
Body Image
Food
Drugs/Alcohol
Personal Holiness
Peace and Quiet
Comfort
Ease
Power
Sleep
Other (list)

Fear

Disapproval
Rejection
Failure
Poverty
Sexual Frustration
Dishonor
Pain
Boredom
Lifelong Singleness/Divorce
Childlessness
A Hard Marriage
Rebellious Children
Physical Hardship
Insecurity
Sickness
Disorder
Obesity
Hunger
Feeling Pain
Messing Up
Chaos
Unrest
Difficulty
Failure
Discomfort
Other (list)

You may recognize a correlation between what you circled under Desire and what you circled under Fear. That is because our flesh operates out of our sinful desires and fears. When we **recognize** what we desire and fear, we are better able to identify them as red flags or indicators of our self-ruled hearts. We can then **repent** of our sin and self-rule, and **return** God to His throne, knowing He is always gracious and forgiving (1 John 1:9).

Control

Once desire has grabbed hold of our heart, we attempt to control people, things, and circumstances. A self-ruled heart, driven by desire, clings to control like a security blanket. In order to obtain that which we believe we must have, we may use intimidation to get the respect we believe we deserve, we may tell a joke to create the attention we long for, or we may pour all our energy into getting the raise or promotion we think will lead to the house, car, or education we want.

On the flip side of the coin, if our self-ruled heart's primary expression is fear, we will control in order to protect. We may use intimidation to keep people from hurting us, tell a joke to avoid vulnerable conversation, or overwork ourselves so we don't lose our job, in order to keep our house, or car, or possessions.[2]

Once we recognize our desires and fears we become more attuned to seeing how we control to obtain or control to protect. Control often manifests itself through guilt, manipulation, intimidation or coercion.

[2] Paraphrased from *Equipped to Counsel* by John Henderson, Second Edition, p. 178.

List ways you use control to obtain what you desire.

List ways you use control to protect
yourself from what you fear.

When our efforts to control the circumstances and/or the people in our lives are successful, our self-ruled heart becomes encouraged to continue on these destructive paths, and arrogance and pride become more deeply rooted. When our efforts are not successful, our prideful, self-ruled heart is discouraged, and we become angry.

Anger

God's word clearly says "for the anger of man does not produce the righteousness of God" (James 1:20). Anger is a red flag that shows us we are operating out of our self-ruled heart. Anger can come in many forms and warns us of impending destruction if we continue on our present course. God's word is clear. Our anger will never achieve—or produce in our circumstances or our relationships—His righteousness. His righteousness is the correct response that will accomplish God's purposes in a given situation. Our anger indicates that something or someone has thwarted our efforts to control to obtain, or control to protect.

Brian and Amy were both very angry. Each of them was thwarting or getting in the way of what the other believed they desperately needed in life to be fulfilled or to be safe, so they saw each other as the enemy and acted accordingly.

Recognizing the Red Flags

A car's dashboard includes a variety of different lights and symbols that light up from time to time. If the system malfunctions, these lights serve as a warning that something is wrong and repairs are necessary. Failing to heed the warning means damage to the vehicle is inevitable.

In the same way, there are red flags or warning lights in our lives that indicate a departure from the way God intended us to live. Some of these early warning signals include unrighteous desires, fears, control, and anger. If we do not heed the warning, we will experience destruction in the circumstances and relationships of our lives.

When you feel anger, it should be a red flag that the crown is on your head and you are ruling your heart. Where do you see these types of responses in your circumstances?

Bondage

The final outcome of self-ruled living is bondage. Trying to control our circumstances by fulfilling our own desires and protecting our fears will ultimately fail. Even if control brings us a measure of success at times, this cycle will ultimately lead to loss of hope, peace, and joy, while birthing feelings of regret, anxiety or depression.

We were not designed to live self-sufficiently. Independence from God leads to a life built on the unstable foundation of human effort and it will collapse when hit by the storms of life. God never intended for us to live in this cycle of bondage. He shows us another way: living with a Christ-ruled heart built on dependence and obedience.

> "Now the works of the flesh are evident: sexual immorality, impurity, sensuality, idolatry, sorcery, enmity, strife, jealousy, fits of anger, rivalries, dissensions, divisions, envy, drunkenness, orgies, and things like these. I warn you, as I warned you before, that those who do such things will not inherit the kingdom of God." –Galatians 5:19-21

A Christ-Ruled Heart

Dependence

> "I am the vine; you are the branches. Whoever abides in me and I in him, he it is that bears much fruit, for apart from me you can do nothing." –John 15:5

Upon our salvation, the Holy Spirit comes to dwell in us and to teach, lead and testify to our hearts that we have been made righteous children of God with all the eternal inheritance and spiritual resources of God available to us (John 14:15-27, John 16:5-15, Romans 8:1-17, Galatians 5:16-26). The idea behind "abide" can be described for the believer as dwelling in a continual state of dependence on God for "life." Practicing a moment-by-moment submission to and dependence on the work of the indwelling Holy Spirit and the external Word of God to give us **all** things that pertain to life and godliness (2 Peter 1:3).

- Submit to the Holy Spirit's word (read and obey the Bible).
- Submit to the Holy Spirit's power (follow the direction in which the Holy Spirit leads us).
- Submit to the Holy Spirit's ministry (allow the Spirit to work in our lives through trials, the influence of the church and being in prayer).

In what ways are you growing in a moment-by moment dependence on God through the Holy Spirit and the Word of God?

Obedience

"But be doers of the word, and not hearers only, deceiving yourselves." – James 1:22-25

Obedience is more than hearing or knowing the Word of God, it is putting into practice what the Word of the God says. Obedience is a moment-by-moment submission to His Word and to His reign in all areas of our thinking, feeling and actions.

The natural response of one who loves God will be the desire to obey.

"Jesus answered him, "If anyone loves me, he will keep my word, and my Father will love him, and we will come to him and make our home with him." – John 14:23

Does your proclamation of your love for God produce obedience to God?

Suffering and Trials

"Beloved, do not be surprised at the fiery trial when it comes upon you to test you, as though something strange were happening to you." –1 Peter 4:12-13

Suffering and trials, while difficult, uncomfortable, and undesirable, are still blessings to us when we are submitted to what God wants to accomplish in our lives. We are not to be surprised that life in a sinful and broken world produces suffering and trials.

What God promises is that He will subjugate that suffering and trial to produce in us His good purposes—ultimately to conform us more and more into the image of His son, Jesus.

God Is in Control

"And we know that for those who love God all things work together for good, for those who are called according to his purpose." –Romans 8:28

God is subjugating all things to his will and forcing them to be good for us in order to produce a steadfast, persevering, hopeful, faithful, joyful faith.

Perseverance and Hope

"Not only that, but we rejoice in our *sufferings*, knowing that suffering produces endurance, and endurance produces character, and character produces hope, and hope does not put us to shame, because God's love has been poured into our hearts through the Holy Spirit who has been given to us." –Romans 5:3-5 (emphasis added)

We can glory (take great pleasure) in our sufferings and trials because we **know** that God is using them to produce in us perseverance. **Perseverance** is not giving up. It is persistence and tenacity, in daily life making the effort needed to do something and keep doing it till the end, even if it's difficult. This is a character quality that God desires to cultivate in his children. The believer who persists even under difficulty is confirming the indwelling of God's Spirt and this produces **hope**.

So we can say with James, we consider it great "joy" when we face various trials, knowing that the testing of our faith will produce steadfastness, firm in belief, determined, and adhering to the work that God is doing in us through the suffering and trial. He is bringing our faith to completion—tested or proved out in the heat of suffering and revealing the internal work of transformation in our heats.

"Count it all joy, my brothers, when you meet trials of various kinds, for you know that the testing of your faith produces steadfastness. And let steadfastness have its full effect, that you may be perfect and complete, lacking in nothing." –James 1:2-4

Freedom

. The result of living in dependence and obedience which is tested and grown in suffering and trials, is trust in God's sovereign control of all of life. This produces in the believer perseverance and hope which leads to freedom found in the person of Jesus who came to set us free (John 8:36). The evidence that we are Christ-ruled in all our life is seen in the fruit that the Holy Spirit produces in us.

"But the fruit of the Spirit is love, joy, peace, patience, kindness, goodness, faithfulness, gentleness, self-control; against such things there is no law." –Galatians 5:22-23

Living Christ-Ruled ensures that our lives will demonstrate the beautiful character of our beloved savior who died for us so that we could truly have LIFE!

Think of times in your life where you have lived self-ruled and other times where have been Christ-ruled. Reflect and journal on the different situations, ways of thinking, and responses during these times.

Death To Me—An Unlikely Blessing

"Death to me..." sounds like a very strange and misguided phrase. But when we really understand its meaning, it becomes a source of freedom and great hope. The only response severe enough to overcome our own self-ruled heart is death. Paul writes in the second chapter of Galatians, "I have been crucified with Christ. It is no longer I who live, but Christ who lives in me. And the life I now live in the flesh I live by faith in the Son of God, who loved me and gave himself for me." (v. 20) We, like Paul, the servant of God and writer of the book of Galatians, identify with Christ's death. Our flesh (self-rule) was nailed to that cross, and there the punishment for sin was paid; our flesh (self-rule) died so that we may be resurrected with Christ to newness of life. It is no longer I who live (self-rule) but rather it is Christ who lives in me (Christ-rule).

This, our death, is now our daily practice! We must intentionally choose to die to our own flesh, our own wicked and deceitful heart, our own self-rule. We must course-correct our thinking and our actions to line up with His word. We must not be ruled by what we think or how we feel but rather live in dependence on and obedience to the living God. In practical terms it means that we choose, every moment of our existence, to live either for our own self or to live for Christ. His will, purpose, and identity become our own only as we put to death our own will, purpose and identity.

God says in His word, "If anyone would come after me, let him deny himself and take up his cross and follow me. For whoever would save his life will lose it, but whoever loses his life for my sake and the gospel's will save it." (Mark 8:34-35)

This is the upside down principal. What makes sense in our self-ruled kingdoms is opposite of what works in the Christ-ruled Kingdom. In Christ's Kingdom, life is found in our choosing death. We easily believe that we can orchestrate and control our circumstances and relationships to bring us life. When we recognize our own self-rule and its destructive nature, we clearly see how its reign will only lead to our destruction. Death to our own self-rule is freedom to live in Christ. May we grasp the beauty of the death of sinful flesh and rejoice in the gift of newness of life.

WHO RULES YOUR HEART?

SELF-RULED
Deceitful. Wicked. (Jeremiah 17:9)

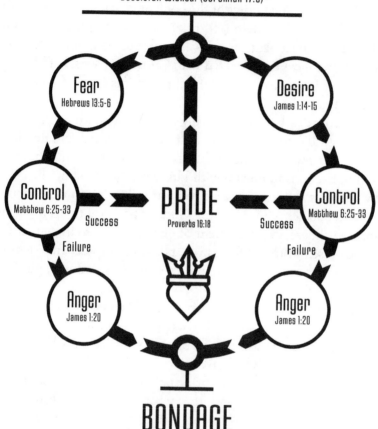

Fear
Hebrews 13:5-6

Desire
James 1:14-15

Control
Matthew 6:25-33

PRIDE
Proverbs 16:18

Control
Matthew 6:25-33

Success

Success

Failure

Failure

Anger
James 1:20

Anger
James 1:20

BONDAGE
Lack of hope. Lack of peace. Lack of joy. Regret. Depression. Anxiety. Addiction

Now the works of the flesh are evident: sexual immorality, impurity, sensuality, idolatry, sorcery, enmity, strife, jealousy, fits of anger, rivalries, dissensions, divisions, envy, drunkenness, orgies, and things like these. I warn you, as I warned you before, that those who do such things will not inherit the kingdom of God. —Galatians 5:19-21

WHO RULES YOUR HEART?

CHRIST-RULED

Christ lives in me. (Galatians 2:20)

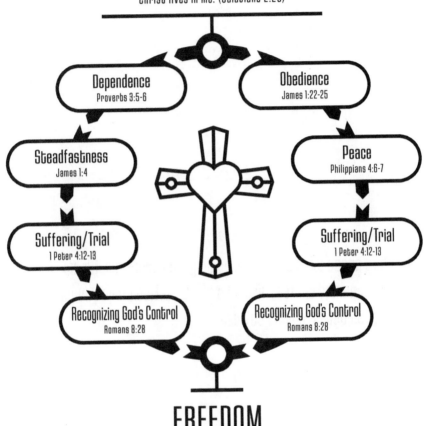

Dependence
Proverbs 3:5-6

Obedience
James 1:22-25

Steadfastness
James 1:4

Peace
Philippians 4:6-7

Suffering/Trial
1 Peter 4:12-13

Suffering/Trial
1 Peter 4:12-13

Recognizing God's Control
Romans 8:28

Recognizing God's Control
Romans 8:28

FREEDOM

Hope. Peace. Joy. Forgiveness. Contentment.

But the fruit of the Spirit is love, joy, peace,
patience, kindness, goodness, faithfulness,
gentleness, self-control; against such
things there is no law. –Galatians 5:22-23

Do you claim to be a follower of Jesus Christ? How then are you denying or putting to death daily your own self-rule?

Identify areas where God is revealing your self-rule. Write these down and confess them to the Lord. List ways you use control to obtain what you desire.

CHAPTER SIX

WHERE'S THE BATTLE?

Our hardest fought battle is not horizontal, but vertical.

Towards the end of World War II, it became apparent that Germany and the Axis forces would be defeated. The final stand was made in Germany's capital city, Berlin, but the Nazis did not surrender without a fight. Their desperate determination to dominate led to the Battle of the Bulge, which was one of the last, and bloodiest, German offensive strikes. Though Hitler's forces were doomed to defeat, they sought to kill and destroy as many allied forces as possible.

Satan's battle plan is similar. Though he was defeated at the cross when Christ died and declared victory over sin and death, he still desires to destroy. He is not yet vanquished. He still reigns over his domain of darkness and evil. His time is limited, so he seeks to spread his carnage throughout the world. Nevertheless, we may take heart, for Jesus has overcome.

As part of our current culture, it is easy for us to confuse the blessing of living in faith with the luxuries of wealth and prosperity. We often convince ourselves that if we acknowledge

God, go to church, and do good things for others, then God will bless our lives with health and wealth. But spiritual blessing looks very different from idealized fulfillment. There are no Scriptures promising a big house, white picket fence, 2.5 kids, and a fuel-efficient SUV. In our pursuit of happiness, we are tempted to create a picture-perfect Christian fantasy based on promises God never made. But the Bible pictures this world more like a war-torn battlefield than a fun-filled amusement park.

How does our outlook change when we begin to see that the world is at war—that we are stationed behind enemy lines?

Doesn't that truth clarify why we see so much pain, suffering, destruction, and death in the world? This is our reality: we may not always see the battle, but we know we have experienced it. We can feel it being waged around us, and when we strive to build a fantasyland of perpetual happiness, we continue to feel cheated when faced with the chaos of suffering. Our perceived reality is shattered, and we cannot make sense of the brokenness around us.

No one expects to build themselves a safe, comfortable, and fulfilling life in the middle of a war zone. The idea is ludicrous.

And yet as believers, we seek comfort and safety from this broken and war-torn world, believing that somehow it will provide the deep joy, peace, and fulfillment our souls are designed for. We know it is available. We can feel the pull of God's redemptive plan. Yet Satan lures us with ease and comfort. He convinces us that chasing self-focused needs will fulfill us, and that the pacifying pleasures of a dying world can bring us comfort.

While we may be tempted to give up hope, the Bible clearly says that for those who trust in Christ, this world is not our home—we are only passing through. God has a mission for us to accomplish and our Chief Commander has not left us defenseless. He gave instructions for how to armor up and live boldly in the war zone, lest we become victims of its deception. God is committed to finishing the work that He started in us on the day of salvation. He will not leave us alone as we wake to the truth of where the real spiritual battle is fought. Instead, He goes before us, guides us, and reminds us to be strong in the strength of His might.

Armor Up!

"Finally, be strong in the Lord and in the strength of His might. Put on the whole armor of God, that you may be able to stand against the schemes of the devil." –Ephesians 6:10-11

Our strength does not come from ourselves, but from God's power of salvation (what Jesus accomplished for us at the cross), the strength of the Holy Spirit (submission to the Spirit), and the force of God's truth (dwelling on God's Word). We must cultivate a right view of God, a submissive heart towards God, and continually be growing in the knowledge of God through His Word. This is how we can be "strong" in the strength of the Lord.

In what ways are you growing in your strength in the Lord?

In what ways will dwelling on God's Word
impact your strength in Christ?

Know the Enemy!

In any war, knowing your enemy is vital. Knowing the way the enemy thinks, his motives, and how he is most likely to attack will help you develop an effective defense. God describes Satan's methods as schemes—referring to the cunning and deceptive philosophies Satan propagates through evil world systems. The current cultural theories of who we are, who God is or is not, how we came to be, and all other similar thoughts that influence us are schemes and outright lies that Satan uses to attack.

Can you identify lies of Satan that are present in your thinking?

"So flee youthful passions and pursue righteousness, faith, love, and peace, along with those who call on the Lord from a pure heart. Have nothing to do with foolish, ignorant controversies; you know that they breed quarrels. And the Lord's servant[a] must not be quarrelsome but kind to everyone, able to teach, patiently enduring evil, correcting his opponents with gentleness. God may perhaps grant them repentance leading to a knowledge of the truth, and they may come to their senses and escape from the snare of the devil, after being captured by him to do his will."
–2 Timothy 2:22-26

Identify areas that you are actually fulfilling the will of Satan in your current situation based on 2 Timothy 2:22-26.

Satan cannot keep us from being saved, but he can make us ineffective at living out our faith by attacking us in these spiritual areas. Satan wants us to doubt God, disobey His boundaries, and refuse to serve Him. He crafts narratives that create division between God, us, and others, and that make us feel comforted and falsely fulfilled, nudging us to bow to our own self-ruled kingdom. The enemy does not care what tactic works best, he is willing to use anything to get us to reject the rule of God in our lives.

Identify the Enemy!

"For we do not wrestle against flesh and blood, but against the rulers, against the authorities, against the cosmic powers over this present darkness, against the spiritual forces of evil in the heavenly places." –Ephesians 6:12

We are often tempted to believe that our most significant battles lie within challenging relationships, handling difficult people, or dealing with unforeseen circumstances. But according to this passage, our most significant struggle is not against "flesh and blood". That challenging relationship with your spouse, ex, parent, coworker, child, or friend is not the real battle, and they are not your real enemy. Satan wants you to believe it, but it's not true. ***Our hardest fought battle is not horizontal, but vertical.*** Satan wants to destroy your relationship with the God of Heaven by selling you the lie that the problem is with your horizontal relationships (those here on Earth).

Which relationships in your life do you believe are part of your current struggle; how have you seen others as the "enemy" in your current circumstances?

Identify areas where you are struggling in your vertical relationship with God and how this is affecting your responses to horizontal relationships.

Don't Doubt!

When Satan attacks, we are tempted to retreat and doubt God's words and character. Our desire for relief can lead to rash decision-making. The tempter convinces us that disobedience can be constructive, that maybe God did not really mean what He said, and that choosing to be self-ruled in our circumstances or relationships is the surest path to satisfaction.

Our wandering hearts (internal compass) ask, "What's the harm?" After biting the hook like a hungry fish, we begin to consider the possibility of living outside the boundaries our good God set in place for our protection. Forsaking wisdom, we greedily pursue sins with high price tags, and we find ourselves sold out to heavy consequences and destruction.

In the chaos and suffering of living, we often doubt God's provision and protection. When we doubt God, we are not seeing Him clearly and we inevitably attempt to find fulfillment in the circumstances and relationships of this world. As a result, sin gains control of our lives and leads us to destruction.

In what areas of your current struggle do you doubt God's provision and protection?

How does your thinking about God's character need to change?

Take Up the Full Armor of God!

"Therefore take up the whole armor of God, that you may be able to withstand in the evil day, and having done all, to stand firm." –Ephesians 6:13

God gives us a practical way to live in the heat of the battle by providing us with His spiritual armor, so we can stand! Let's investigate what His provisions and protection look like for a soldier in the war zone.

Again, we see that our struggle is a spiritual battle being fought by the agents and rulers of darkness (Satan and his cohort) in the heavenly places. Because of this truth, we are to "take up the full armor of God," enabling us to both resist and to stand firm in the face of evil and temptation. God, as our sovereign protector, offers instruction on how to live in the midst of the war.

Like any good soldier, we must always be prepared. We never know what attacks may come our way as we engage in battle. God directs us to "take up" or "put on" the appropriate armor and gear that we need for our protection and benefit. It is this "putting on" that enables us to both resist (not give into the temptation) and to stand (not to be knocked down or run over) against the evil of this world.

A Roman soldier was issued a set of items, armor, that he was expected to wear. In the same way, as an active solider in the Kingdom, we are to daily "put on" the spiritual armor that God provides. This should be a Christian's permanent spiritual attire. A wise soldier would never enter a battlefield without appropriate gear for protection and defense. We too need protection—our spiritual armor.

Let's consider the specific pieces of armor we are to "put on" daily.

What does "putting on the full armor of God"
look like in your daily life?

In which areas are you tempted to fall into retreat and or defeat?

Stand Firm!

"Stand therefore, having fastened on the belt of truth, and having put on the breastplate of righteousness." –Ephesians 6:14

God does not repeat Himself without purpose, and this is the third time in this passage that we are instructed to "stand firm". We must hold our position in this spiritual combat, and God provides the means. Consider the four areas we are to "Be" about each day in order to stand, and answer the following questions.

Describe how you remain standing in battle:

In what ways are you being knocked down?

What changes do you need to make to "stand" in your circumstances?

Put On The Belt of Truth!

After following the command to stand, we are instructed to fasten on the belt of truth, God's Word. At first this may sound a bit strange or even awkward, but the Roman soldiers were a very present force in the time the apostles were planting churches, including the one in Ephesus. They daily put on tunics as a part of their uniform. During these times, before guns and aircrafts, much of the military action took place in close combat. If the fighters were not careful to gird up any loose ends of their tunic into their belt in preparation for battle, they could give the enemy a deadly advantage. Likewise, we are to gather in all the loose thinking that trips us up and wrap it in truth, so that wrong or unbiblical thinking does not become a hindrance to our ability to hold our ground. We must identify unbiblical thinking and replace it with biblical truth.

Identify two areas of unbiblical thinking you
have about your current situation.

What biblical truth can you replace your unbiblical thinking with?

Put on the Breastplate of Righteousness!

In practice, we put on righteousness by living in obedience to God's Word and in dependence on His Spirit. Just as the commander of a great army gives instructions to his soldiers to follow, so too, the Living God gives us clear instructions through His Word. The purpose of the instructions is to accomplish stated goals and objectives as well as to protect the soldiers from harm. A wise commander creates in his soldiers a healthy dependence on his leadership and abilities. Each soldier grows in relationship with the commander as he serves faithfully under his rule.

Likewise, we grow in our dependence on, and in our relationship with, the Living God as He leads us through the embattled terrain of this life. The more we see Him as all-wise, powerful, good, just and loving, the more we grow in obedience and dependence on His rule in our lives.

"As we learn to live in obedience to and in fellowship with Jesus Christ, His righteousness will produce in us a practical righteousness that becomes our spiritual breastplate." (John MacArthur Study Bible p. 1784, 2006)

Our obedience and dependence shapes and informs our thinking, feelings and actions. We think, feel and act more like the Living God as we bring our thoughts, feelings and actions into alignment with Christ. In other words we will think, feel and act more like the Living God than ourselves. This is how we can expect to "stand" against the attack of the enemy in the midst of the fray.

How are you securing the breastplate of righteousness through practicing obedience and daily fellowship?

Live Gospel-Centered!

"…as shoes for your feet, having put on the readiness given by the gospel of peace." –Ephesians 6:15

Living in the constant presence and reality of the Gospel, the good news of salvation that was purchased for us by the blood of Jesus Christ, cements a peace that surpasses understanding. God's grace, extended through His Son, brought peace between God and His creation. This enables us to go boldly before God's throne of grace to receive His mercy. These truths bring stability in an unstable and hostile environment. The Gospel is not a one-time soundbite but a continual rehearsal of what Christ did for us. Out of that flows our growing dependence on, and obedience to, the one who died to give us life. The Gospel is central to everything!

Share the Gospel in your own words.

What part does the Gospel message play in your life?

Take up The Shield of Faith!

"In all circumstances take up the shield of faith, with which you can extinguish all the flaming darts of the evil one." –Ephesians 6:16

No ancient soldier would have been ready for the horrors of war without a shield. By taking up the shield of faith, you guard not only your heart and body but also your mind. This refers to the believer's dependence and trust in God's Word and His promises. God's truth becomes a safeguard against the fiery arrows of the evil one. These arrows create doubt about God and His faithfulness, wound and poison our view of God's wisdom, and cripple our ability to act with power and strength in our lives.

Satan aims at the tender areas of our faith and releases sharp lies in hopes they will break through our protection. God's truth will prevail, and it is the only defense that will shield us from the evil one's persistent attacks.

How do you put the defensive tool of trust in God's faithfulness and promises into daily practice?

List three of God's promises that will fortify your thinking in your current circumstances.

Put on the Helmet of Salvation!

"...And take the helmet of salvation..." –Ephesians 6:17a

A cunning enemy knows to shoot for the heart or strike at the head. A solid blow to the head can alter the very way a brain works. The helmet was designed to protect this vulnerable area. Its purpose was to deflect deadly blows. In the same way, the helmet of salvation protects our minds with the promise of security in Christ. It is meant to be a source of assurance in what Christ has done for us, a reminder of our true identity. When we are confident that He is God, that we are His, and that He has saved us, we approach the battlefield not in fear, but with the fortitude of one who knows victory is assured.

How does the truth of your salvation bring
you confidence and steadfastness?

What truths of the Gospel do you need to grow in?

Take Up the Sword!

"...And the sword of the Spirit, which is the word of God..."
–Ephesians 6:17b

The sword of the Spirit is the one offensive weapon included in a soldier's full armor. A seasoned swordsman is powerful, but skill requires practice. Skills are sharpened and proficiency increased through daily discipline. The believer must be fully trained and equipped to wield the Word effectively against the attacks of the enemy, as well as to help destroy the strategies and schemes of Satan.

God's word is the weapon Jesus used when the devil tempted Him (Luke 4:1-13). With it, Jesus cut through every temptation. The power and might of what God had already spoken is the power that demolishes the enemy's fortified places and strongholds. The Word of God also holds a mirror to the sin in our lives, so that we may repent and be set free. It is able to detect and destroy spiritual strongholds and break through and replace the hardness sin has caused in our hearts.

How are you practicing the skillful use of the Word of God to expose and destroy areas of sin and unrighteousness in your life?

How are you practicing the skillful use of the Word of God to expose and destroy the attacks of Satan and stay free from the trappings of this world?

CHAPTER SEVEN

WHY SUFFERING?

The answer to our current suffering is not to try and change or remove the trial, but to allow the living God to fundamentally change how we think about our trials.

A diamond is a beautiful thing! Highly prized and greatly valued for its brilliance and light, it is easy to forget that a diamond must go through intense pressure, time, and chiseling before its value and beauty can be displayed.

Faith is like a diamond in the rough, and our God is willing to patiently bring forth its beauty. He, being the master craftsman, chisels away at our impurities (sin). For only with perfect and controlled cuts can our faith adequately reflect the light and brilliance of God's holy and redeeming love in our lives.

Though suffering was not present in the first days of creation, it entered as a result of the first couple's sin. As a result, we see broken lives struggling in a broken world. Sin clearly brings destruction.

A tool in the hand of the destroyer (Satan)—not the craftsman (our God)—sin ultimately creates suffering, pain, and loss. And the terrifying truth is that we all feel it. The good news is that sin's hold on us is broken, and we are set free when we place our faith in the work of Jesus on the cross.

He became sin on our behalf so we would no longer be enslaved to it (2 Corinthians 5:21). But this doesn't mean we won't feel the consequences of our indulgence. On this cursed planet, we may always struggle with indwelling sin, but by His grace we now have the ability to *recognize*, *repent* and *replace* Christ back on the throne as ruler of our lives.

The living God now creates purpose and meaning through suffering whether it is a consequence of living under general sin—the sin of a broken and lost world—or the consequences of our specific wrong choices. God not only forgives, He faithfully uses these consequences—pain, and suffering—to grow us and shape us into His Son's image.

God's purpose in our lives now is to deal with our remaining sin, which is our greatest problem, even though we seldom recognize it as such. God permits pressure and difficulties to eliminate sin and create in us a refined and treasured faith. As our great soul-smith, He desires to chisel away the impurities revealing a life made like that of Christ. He uncovers the places we have hidden, not to disgrace us, but to release us.

Identifying our trials and sufferings as tools of the master craftsman produces hope. The darkness of affliction allows His image reflected in us to shine all the more brightly. Now *that* is a God we can fully trust—a God who walks with us into all our circumstances, and a God who redeems our suffering by creating character in us. A God who sweeps away the dross that has collected on our faith and makes us a radiant reflection of His glory! This is our craftsman, our soul-smith—our God!

How we think about suffering, biblically or unbiblically, greatly effects how our trial impacts our lives. **We cannot change the trial but we can change how we think about the trial and that changes how we experience it.**

Complete *Unbiblical Thinking* (p. 107) to get a clearer picture of what may be keeping you from fully reflecting God in your life.

UNBIBLICAL THINKING

Part A

What influences how you think about your suffering?

Family, parent, coworker, neighbor, media, music, personal prejudices…

Describe the trial you are currently experiencing.

Explain how this trial affects you.

Conflict, finances, parenting, ability to function or think clearly,…

Note how this trial affects your feelings.

Feeling overwhelmed, wronged, hopeless, angry, fearful, numb, forgotten,…

Consider these biblical truths about suffering and how it impacts how we think about and experience suffering:

- Suffering is the inevitable byproduct of living in a broken and sinful world.
- Suffering is normal.
- Suffering is the means God uses to expose what our heart desires/fears.
- Suffering is the means God uses to reveal our need for deeper dependence and obedience.
- Suffering does not cause us to sin.

We experience suffering for many reasons:

- Social circumstances (i.e., death in the family, broken relationships, betrayal by friends)
- The condition of our soul (i.e., spiritually unhealthy choices)
- Our physical bodies (i.e., physical and mental disease and disorders)
- The torment of demons
- Our own sinful choices (i.e., abuse, cultivating habits that lead to addiction)
- Natural disasters ("Acts of God")
- The sinful choices of others (i.e., persecution, spousal abuse)

Describe your current circumstance and what is causing suffering in your life:

Not All Suffering is Bad

God uses all things for the good of those who love Him (Romans 8:28). The testing of our faith develops perseverance. Perseverance leads to our maturing and being made complete in our faith (James 1). Therefore, the sooner we learn to consider suffering as joy because of what it produces in us, the sooner God can use our suffering to conform us into the image of His Son, and the sooner we may bear His image well.

God Reveals a Biblical Example of Suffering

God gives us an incredible picture of suffering in the Old Testament book of Job. It is God's account of one of His own faithful image-bearers who loved Him and served Him. But God did not keep pain and suffering from Job's life.

The scene opens in Heaven where Satan comes into God's presence after roaming Earth. God tells Satan to consider His servant Job. Satan mocks. He's sure Job only loves and serves God because of His blessing. If those blessings were removed, Job would surely curse God.

Satan wanted to prove that faith in God is tied only to the experience of protection, prosperity and comfort. So Satan challenged God to test Job's faith. God gave His sovereign permission for Satan to attack "all that he has" (Job 1:12).

Job experienced suffering in unimaginable ways. He lost everything, including his health and nearly everyone dear to him. In pain and suffering, Job wrestled with his lack of understanding of what God was doing in his life, and he questioned God's wisdom and His justice.

Isn't that exactly what we do in our pain and suffering? We begin to question God's wisdom; does He really know what He is doing? How can this be His plan? Like Job, we also are quick to question His justice by saying, "This is not fair. How could God allow this after all I have done for Him?" We easily begin to doubt God and question His character. We slip into defining God through the circumstances. If my life is good, God is good. If my life is bad, God is bad.

How have you experienced doubt in God's presence or questioned God's character in your suffering?

God Reveals Himself in Our Suffering

God lovingly humbled Job by asking him a series of questions: "Job, where were you when I laid the foundations of the earth… Have you understood the expanse of the earth…" and on and on. In the end, Job was done questioning and challenging God's wisdom and His justice. Job was humbled and crushed beneath the weighty truth of God's greatness and majesty. Without answers to all of his questions, Job quietly bowed in submission to his Creator and His plan for Job's life. He ends with these profound words; "I have heard of you by the hearing of the ear; but now my eye sees you…" (Job 42:5).

In the midst of Job's suffering, God revealed Himself. Not on Job's terms, and not through God being defined by how Job would like him to be (a god of his own making), but, in the middle of his pain, Job experienced the living God. He had heard of Him, knew Him in a limited way, but now he had a greater understanding of God's power, majesty, and greatness, and this truth brought peace to Job's heart.

In what ways has God used suffering to expand your knowledge and understanding of Him?

Notice Job is never given the context or reason for his suffering. We often think that if we could just understand the purpose or the reason for our suffering, we could deal with it. God, however, through Scripture, clearly tells us that He and He alone authors peace in our heart and mind in the midst of our pain and suffering. God uses our trials to reveal Himself.

Are you seeking reasons for your suffering? Write out some possible explanations for your suffering.

Now ask yourself, "Can I still trust God without knowing the reason?"

In what ways do you see God as the peace and comfort you desire and not the reason for your suffering?

What do you need to change in your thinking so you're able to see Him as the answer to your current need?

God Reveals Our Need for Growth in Our Suffering

God is committed to completing the work He began in us at salvation through the process of sanctification. Sanctification is our spiritual growth, and God uses the relationships and the circumstances of our lives as a means of growing us.

The trials of life, our circumstances and our relationships become the context in which the content of our heart is revealed. God knows our heart better than we do. Revealing our heart-rule is His gracious and loving way of showing us where we are deceived and choosing bondage to sin instead of freedom. He desires us to live in dependent obedience to Him and experience the profound joy He promises, even in the midst of suffering.

He uses trials and suffering to test who is really on the throne of our heart. Once we *recognize* our self-rule, we then have opportunity to *repent* of our self-rule, and our rebellion against our reigning King, and *replace* Him onto that throne.

What do your current circumstances reveal about who is ruling your heart?

God Reveals Our Sin in Our Suffering

In the same way that the diamond requires great amounts of pressure over long periods of time, our faith also requires pressure and time to move us from self-rule to Christ-rule. Our master soul-smith carefully chisels away the impurities (sin) that diminish the beauty and brilliance of our faith.

Some of the impurities that are revealed in the process become evident in our lives during suffering. Our self-ruled heart will always produce ungodly responses to our suffering.

Consider What God Says in His Word

"Now the works of the flesh are evident: sexual immorality, impurity, sensuality, idolatry, sorcery, enmity, strife, jealousy, fits of anger, rivalries, dissensions, divisions, envy, drunkenness, orgies, and things like these." –Galatians 5:19-21a

When we are hurting, we respond in all types of ways. Maybe we choose envy, looking with longing at others' lives that we perceive are easier or richer than ours. Or perhaps we numb ourselves with sexual distractions or alcohol or food. Will we become angry, irritable, quarrelsome and difficult to be around? Or choose to throw a pity party then isolate from or degrade those who refuse to join?

God desires to reveal what is hidden in our hearts because He wants us free from the indwelling sin that blocks us from fellowship with Him and from experiencing the abundant life He died to give us.

Read again through the list in Galatians 5:19-21a.

Which acts of the flesh are obvious in your life that God is lovingly revealing to you in the midst of your suffering?

God Reveals His Comfort in Our Suffering

God understands the horrific pain and overwhelming weightiness of suffering that lays hold of our souls and at times drowns our very existence in fear and grief. And remember,

God did not spare His own son from that experience. God also allowed Jesus to suffer all things so that He could comfort us unlike any other (see 2 Corinthians 1:3-5).

There is only One who knows and truly understands our deepest sorrow and who is capable of comforting our soul. There is no earthly comfort like comfort from the living God. He will speak to our hurt through His Word and minister His sweet healing power in our circumstances. We must continually seek His comfort through prayer and His Word. In this way He ministers to our souls.

Make a list of how you plan to intentionally set your thoughts on the truth of who God is and the comfort of His presence.

What commitment are you willing to make to regularly turn to God's Word and prayer for comfort (and everything else)?

God Reveals Unbiblical Thinking in Our Suffering

How we think about suffering (biblically/unbiblically) greatly affects how our trial impacts our lives. We cannot change the trial but we can change how we think about the trial and that changes how we experience it. We often want God or others to change our circumstances or relationships to give us release or relief from our suffering. But God's Word has been faithful throughout history.

Jesus, in words we don't typically post on our refrigerators and bathroom mirrors, said, "In this world you will have tribulation" (John 16:33). Peter echoes that promise, "Do not be surprised at the fiery trial when it comes upon you" (1 Peter 4:12). A biblical understanding of suffering instructs us to expect trials, difficulty, pain and suffering. It's one part of our human experience here on Earth we can count on.

We must recognize that the real problem is not the trial. Rather, it's how we think about the trial that impacts our lives. This is good news, since often we have no control over the world around us, for good or ill. However, we do have the ability to choose and control how we think about and respond to our trials. We choose whether to think about them biblically or unbiblically.

God provides great promises to those who love Him and who walk through trials in obedience to His directions. *So the answer to our current suffering is not to try and change or remove the trial, but to allow the living God to fundamentally change how we think about our trials.*

We are told to consider it "joy" when we experience trials and suffering. (James 1) The word implies that we are to think about suffering in a specific way. Scripture is clear that in choosing to consider our trials as "joy," our experience of suffering changes.

Now that you have worked through the truths of God's Word on suffering, complete Part B of *Biblical Thinking*. (p. 120) Answer the same questions, but now from a biblical perspective.

Notice how the way we think about suffering (biblically/ unbiblically) greatly affects how our trial impacts our lives. We cannot change the trial, but we can change how we think about the trial, and that changes how we experience it.

BIBLICAL THINKING

Part B

How does Biblical thinking change your view of your suffering?

Describe the trial you are currently experiencing.

Explain how biblical thinking affects you.

Note how biblical thinking affects your feelings.

CHAPTER EIGHT

WHO IS YOUR FOUNDATION?

A house built on solid rock can withstand the effects of any storm.

You may not have given it much thought, but you have often benefitted from the planning and construction of a well-built structure. When we walk into a home, a shopping complex, or a hospital, we don't often reflect on the multiple layers needed to create such a space. We may notice the exterior and interior architecture, or be inspired by the function the structure provides, but all buildings, whether great or small, have one important component that impacts their effectiveness, appearance, and longevity. We walk over it, but our attention is not drawn to it. It's the behind-the-scenes workhorse of every successful construction project—the foundation.

Though it may appear a simple part of the overall development process, setting the foundation correctly is incredibly important. Any shortcuts, cracks, or flaws affect the whole structure, and the impact of imperfections worsens progressively as the building rises. The term for this type of issue is *compounding defects*, because if you make mistakes in the foundation, the problems that follow are compounded. These will be seen and felt throughout the building, affecting both structure and appearance.

Our spiritual lives are similar; errors in our foundation create compounding defects as we attempt to grow. Jesus tells us in Luke 6:46-49 that we are to build our house upon a rock. If we are not anchored to the rock, Jesus, then all further maturation in our lives will be impacted by compounding defects that leave us vulnerable to the storms of life.

If we are building a spiritual house on a foundation anchored to our own thoughts, worldly wisdom, concepts, or ideas, then we can expect to find weakness. A foundation established with ourselves as the rock will contain mistakes because no one but Christ is perfect. When we build apart from Him, we build upon shifting beliefs instead of eternal truths. This will compound. What we choose as our foundation determines the structural integrity of our faith.

> "Why do you call me 'Lord, Lord,' and not do what I tell you? Everyone who comes to me and hears my words and does them, I will show you what he is like: he is like a man building a house, who dug deep and laid the foundation on the rock. And when a flood arose, the stream broke against that house and could not shake it, because it had been well built. But, the one who hears and does not do them is like a man who built a house on the ground without a foundation. When the stream broke against it, immediately it fell, and the ruin of that house was great." –Luke 6:46-47

Following the Instructions

"Everyone who comes to me and hears my words and does them…" –Luke 6:47a

A foreman must precisely follow the architect's plans. Taking instruction from the blueprints and paying careful attention to details, the contractor who lays the foundation meticulously, avoids the frustration of compounding defects. In the same way, God has given specific instructions, a blueprint, for how we should live. If we build according to those instructions, we can expect to experience the beauty and structural soundness of a faith that withstands difficulty, pressure, and challenges from the storms of this life. A spiritual foundation crafted with obedience will build a life free from the compounding effects of sin.

Do you spend time in the Bible? What does it look like for you to be obedient to God's Word?

The Wise Builder

"Everyone who comes to me and hears my words and does them, I will show you what he is like..." –Luke 6:47

Relating to those surrounding Him, Jesus paints a verbal picture of what a person who wants to be His disciple (follower/ student) looks like. Notice how the passage connects those who come to Him ("followers"), with those who hear and obey ("disciples"). Obedience is the key ingredient to building a foundation on Jesus Christ.

In what areas do you struggle with obedience?

The Foundation

"He is like a man building a house, who dug deep and laid the foundation on the rock..." –Luke 6:48a

The word picture Jesus paints for us here is one of a person who is in the process of building a house. Pay close attention to where he chooses to lay the foundation: on solid rock. Jesus is emphasizing the importance of a stable, unshifting base on which to build. This understructure provides support, upholding the home when the torrents of life rain down. Our spiritual lives must be built on the chief "cornerstone" Jesus. He is the understructure for all of our spiritual growth.

What are you building your spiritual foundation upon?

The Storms of Life

"…And when a flood arose, the stream broke against that house and could not shake it…" –Luke 6:48b

Storms represent the small trials we face daily (cloudbursts), the major events which invade less often (hurricanes) and every difficulty with relationships and circumstances in between. Storms reveal the strengths and weaknesses in our foundation: "When the tempest passes, the wicked is no more, but the righteous is established forever." –Proverbs 10:25

What are some of the storms you are facing now?

What is your storm revealing about your foundation?

A Well Built Foundation

"…Because it had been well built." –Luke 6:48c

A house built on solid rock can withstand anything the weather throws at it. The stability of the foundation—the rock—ensures it is grounded and sound, so its inhabitants can live in security. Our spiritual life must, in the same way, be built on the stable foundation of the truth of who God is. Dependence on, and obedience to, His guidance and instruction allows the Spirit to produce perseverance, hope, and joy as we follow His plans for us. Obeying Him in love, we find that our faith endures the many attacks and torrents of living in this fallen world. He is truly our Rock and our Salvation!

If storms have left your life a pile of wreckage, what changes do you need to make to rebuild your life on the "Rock" Christ?

If your life has weathered the current storm of life, give thanks to your faithful Rock and Foundation.

Recognize areas of potential growth as the storms test your spiritual steadfastness.

The Foolish Builder

"But the one who hears and does not do them is like a man who built a house on the ground without a foundation. When the stream broke against it, immediately it fell…" –Luke 6:49

When we encounter the truth, instructions, or information that we need yet choose not to act on or obey, we are fools. We knowingly make choices that lead to destruction. If we are clearly informed about the importance of building our spiritual lives on the foundation of God's truth, and yet choose to actively disobey the directives, we will suffer the consequences. We are welcoming destruction into our house and our lives, and the ruin will be more than we want (or need) to bear.

What are you hearing from the Word of God in your life?

How are you actively choosing to obey what you hear?

What is the status of your spiritual structure?
How has it stood the test of the storms of life?

The Compounding Effects of Sin

"...And the ruin of that house was great." –Luke 6:49b

Sin causes cracks in the foundation of our lives. If not corrected, these will produce compounding sin in our future. We have all seen romantic movies about a couple who meet under the pretense of mistaken identity. We watch with anticipation the princess disguised as a housemaid, the street thief posing as a prince, or the superhero disguised as a mild-mannered news reporter. The plot thickens as they continue to build a relationship founded on a charade of omissions and deceit. The tangled web of lies becomes more complex and intertwined. One lie leads to another until the whole structure of their lives comes crashing down, and only the truth is left, mixed with feelings of hurt. While the destruction was inevitable, healing is still possible. Jesus and His Truth is the solid foundation on which an unshakeable life can be built.

WHO IS YOUR FOUNDATION?

What compounding effects of sin do you recognize in your current circumstances and relationships (conflict, destructive choices and relationships, instability, increasing problems, increasing conflict and difficulty)?

What changes do you need to make in order to correct the compounding defects (sin) in your life?

The marker on this journey shows us that our faith can withstand the effects of a storm because it has been built on solid rock. The stability of the foundation—the rock—ensures it is grounded and sound, that our faith is secure on the journey. Our spiritual life must, in the same way, be built on the stable foundation of the truth of who God is. Dependence on, and obedience to, His guidance and instruction will allow the Spirit to produce peace, joy, and love as we follow the path He has laid out for us. Obeying Him in love, we find that our faith endures the many attacks and torrents of living in this fallen world. He is truly our Rock and our Salvation! Follow well!

CHAPTER NINE

HOW DO I CHANGE?

Conclusion

"I have said these things to you, that in me you may have peace. In the world you will have tribulation. But take heart; I have overcome the world." –John 16:33

"Beloved, do not be surprised at the fiery trial when it comes upon you to test you, as though something strange were happening to you. But rejoice insofar as you share Christ's sufferings, that you may also rejoice and be glad when his glory is revealed." –1 Peter 4:12-13

"In this you rejoice, though now for a little while, if necessary, you have been grieved by various trials…" –1 Peter 1:6

While we have come to the end of *this* journey, your journey with Christ will continue throughout your lifetime. Together, we have learned that the storms of life come in the form of difficulties we face in circumstances and in relationships—suffering and pain, conflict and discord, tragedy and loss. Storms are fixtures in our broken world. They come at inconvenient times and with varying severity. Everyone is affected. They may approach with the power of a tsunami, or they may come as a mist of misfortune among the mundane of everyday living (1 Peter 4:12). Storms are a certainty on our journey, and how we respond—either with a self-ruled or Christ-ruled heart—makes all the difference. In this last chapter we will examine the chart (See *How Do I Change* on p. 151) to explore what it looks like to navigate a storm both from a self-ruled and a Christ-ruled heart.

A Self-Ruled Approach to Trials and Suffering

"Self-Examination"

"There is a way that seems right to a man, but its end is the way to death." –Proverbs 16:25

"For, being ignorant of the righteousness of God, and seeking to establish their own, they did not submit to God's righteousness." –Romans 10:3

When we are self-ruled, we view our self and trial based on our own desires, fears, expectations or perceptions.

In what ways can you identify with this type of approach?

"See to it that no one takes you captive by philosophy and empty deceit, according to human tradition, according to the elemental spirits of the world, and not according to Christ."
–Colossians 2:8

Identify philosophies and ideas from the world that might have influenced your thinking and actions:

"Unbiblical Response"

"If you do well, will you not be accepted? And if you do not do well, sin is crouching at the door. Its desire is contrary to you, but you must rule over it." –Genesis 4:7

When we view our circumstances through our own self-examination, not relying on God's Word, our reactions and responses will be unbiblical.

What unbiblical responses have you found yourself defaulting to?

In Genesis 4:7, *"If you do what is right"* refers to obedience. God counsels Cain, encouraging him to choose obedience.

In what areas do you sense God's Spirit speaking to your spirit, wanting your obedience to His word in your circumstances?

The verse includes a warning: If you will not obey, then sin is crouching, like a lion, at your door and it desires to rule you.

Think of examples of how sin acts like a lion that is ready to pounce and devour you:

According to this verse, what is the remedy for, or the protection from, the sin that desires to overtake you?

"Practice Sin"

"Jesus answered them, 'Truly, truly, I say to you, everyone who practices sin is a slave to sin.'" –John 8:34

When we don't practice obedience in our trials then we choose to practice sin. A self-ruled heart will practice sin.

Sin feels like a freedom we indulge in, when in reality it's a master we serve. Jesus died for our sins to give us freedom from bondage to its power.

"Little children, let no one deceive you. Whoever practices righteousness is righteous, as he is righteous. Whoever makes a practice of sinning is of the devil, for the devil has been sinning from the beginning. The reason the Son of God appeared was to destroy the works of the devil. No one born of God makes a practice of sinning, for God's seed abides in him; and he cannot keep on sinning, because he has been born of God." –1 John 3:7-9

God's Word is clear. If we are His children, then our bondage to sin is broken. We should experience the conviction and guilt of sin along with an internal desire to grow in His righteousness, because He dwells in us. If we continue to practice sin, we must investigate our own heart to see if we are truly His child.

In your current circumstances where were you— or where might you still—be practicing sin?

"Increased Problems"

"But each person is tempted when he is lured and enticed by his own desire. Then desire when it has conceived gives birth to sin, and sin when it is fully grown brings forth death." –James 1:14-15

Life is full of temptations—what the world, through Satan, promises will give us "life"—that prey on our desires and fears. When we grab hold of temptation, lust and sin are born. Sin always leads to death—ultimately physical death—and in the course of our lives sin will be the death of hope, peace, perseverance, friendship, love and a myriad of other blessings God intended for our pleasure. Sin always increases and compounds itself unless we kill it by recognizing it, repenting and confessing it to God, and replacing it with thinking and behavior consistent with the righteousness that is ours in Christ Jesus.

"Bondage"

"Now the works of the flesh are evident: sexual immorality, impurity, sensuality, idolatry, sorcery, enmity, strife, jealousy, fits of anger, rivalries, dissensions, divisions, envy, drunkenness, orgies, and things like these. I warn you, as I warned you before, that those who do such things will not inherit the kingdom of God." –Galatians 5:19-21

The final outcome of living self-ruled is bondage. Living out of fear and desire, seeking to constantly control—even while experiencing some occasional measures of success—ultimately fails. We are left with internal bitterness and anger, deprived of what we thought we were entitled to achieve. God did not design us to live independently or self-sufficiently. The consequences of attempting to fulfill our own desires or to protect ourselves from what we fear, apart from Him, always leads to bondage in a life we have built on the unstable foundation of human effort. When the storms of life come, they bring our life crashing down into a sea of anxiety, depression, addiction and destruction. The evidence, or fruit, of a self-ruled life is easily identified. Our wrongful worship of self produces the fruit of fleshy behaviors God's Word warns us of.

A Christ-Ruled Approach to Trials and Suffering

"Biblical Examination"

"Examine yourselves, to see whether you are in the faith. Test yourselves. Or do you not realize this about yourselves, that Jesus Christ is in you?—unless indeed you fail to meet the test!" –2 Corinthians 13:5

"Search me, O God, and know my heart! Try me and know my thoughts!" –Psalm 139:23

A Christ-ruled approach to trials and suffering begins with a biblical view of yourself and your trial.

In what ways has the Word of God (the Bible) shaped how you face your trial?

"Biblical Response"

"All Scripture is breathed out by God and profitable for teaching, for reproof, for correction, and for training in righteousness, that the man of God may be complete, equipped for every good work." –2 Timothy 3:16-17

The biblical response to our trials recognizes the truths of God's Word. God reveals Himself through the pages of Scripture which His Spirit uses to guide, comfort, encourage and correct us. The Word of God is an incredible gift to us. The more we marinate in His Word, the more it shapes our thinking and our response to trials.

In what ways does knowing Jesus and His Word shape your thinking and your responses to God, self and others in your trial?

"Practice Obedience"

...By Becoming a Doer of the Word:

"But be doers of the word, and not hearers only, deceiving yourselves. For if anyone is a hearer of the word and not a doer, he is like a man who looks intently at his natural face in a mirror. For he looks at himself and goes away and at once forgets what he was like. But the one who looks into the perfect law, the law of liberty, and perseveres, being no hearer who forgets but a doer who acts, he will be blessed in his doing." –James 1:22-25

When we face a trial and we are Christ-ruled, we can practice obedience to God's word. As any professional athlete will attest, practice requires time and dedication. Though we don't often get it right the first time, with practice we become better at thinking and responding in a biblical way.

What do you find most difficult when practicing obedience?

How is God's Word foundational for understanding how to practice obedience?

According to James 1:25, what will bring blessing into your trial?

...By Putting Off the Old and Putting on the New:

"...To put off your old self, which belongs to your former manner of life and is corrupt through deceitful desires, and to be renewed in the spirit of your minds, and to put on the new self, created after the likeness of God in true righteousness and holiness. Therefore, having put away falsehood, let each one of you speak the truth with his neighbor, for we are members one of another. Be angry and do not sin; do not let the sun go down on your anger, and give no opportunity to the devil. Let the thief no longer steal, but rather let him labor, doing honest work with his own hands, so that he may have something to share with anyone in need. Let no corrupting talk come out of your mouths, but only such as is good for building up, as fits the occasion, that it may give grace to those who hear. And do not grieve the Holy Spirit of God, by whom you were sealed for the day of redemption. Let all bitterness and wrath and anger and clamor and slander be put away from you, along with all malice. Be kind to one another, tenderhearted, forgiving one another, as God in Christ forgave you." –Ephesians 4:22-32

Ephesians 4:22-32 is one example of how to obey the Word of God by "putting off" and "putting on." Our days are made of thousands of choices between being Christ-ruled and being self-ruled. The chart below shows how God graciously provides not just a list of what we're to put off, but a list of what we can put on as well.

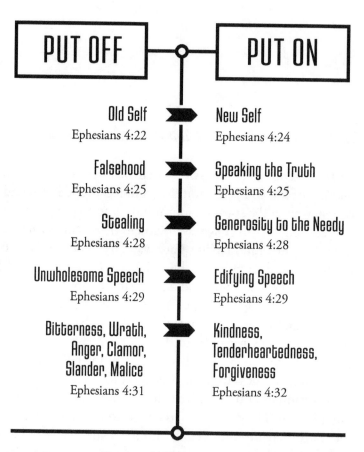

PUT OFF	PUT ON
Old Self Ephesians 4:22	New Self Ephesians 4:24
Falsehood Ephesians 4:25	Speaking the Truth Ephesians 4:25
Stealing Ephesians 4:28	Generosity to the Needy Ephesians 4:28
Unwholesome Speech Ephesians 4:29	Edifying Speech Ephesians 4:29
Bitterness, Wrath, Anger, Clamor, Slander, Malice Ephesians 4:31	Kindness, Tenderheartedness, Forgiveness Ephesians 4:32

Bitterness	Anger and disappointment at being treated unfairly; resentment.
Anger	A strong feeling of annoyance, displeasure, or hostility.
Rage/Wrath	Violent, uncontrolled anger.
Slander	The action or crime of making a false spoken statement damaging to a person's reputation.
Malice	The desire to harm someone; ill will.

Which of the old self's behaviors do you identify in your own life?

Once you **recognize** those behaviors in your life, you must biblically put them off—**repent**—since they are a product of a self-ruled heart. Then **replace** them with biblical responses that come from a heart ruled by Christ.

In what ways do you see the Spirit producing biblical responses in your new self as you yield in dependence and obedience to Christ's rule in your life?

Increased Growth

"But grow in the grace and knowledge of our Lord and Savior Jesus Christ." –2 Peter 3:18

"Therefore, as you received Christ Jesus the Lord, so walk in him, rooted and built up in him and established in the faith, just as you were taught, abounding in thanksgiving." –Colossians 2:6-7

Practicing obedience to God's ways will lead to growth in our relationship with Him and leads to a lasting change.

What will it look like in your life when you "walk in Him"?

What specific practices (new habits) will you put into place to grow in your love for and obedience to God?

Freedom

"So if the Son sets you free, you will be free indeed." –John 8:36

Jesus provided the means for us to live in freedom. It is not found in the circumstances and/or the relationships we experience here on Earth. It is found in relationship with our living God through the person of Jesus. This freedom allows us to live a life that produces peace, joy, and contentment in our circumstances.

In what ways is the presence of Jesus is your life obvious?

"Follow Me"

The path through life is sometimes hard, confusing, overwhelming and chaotic. Jesus has a simple (though not always easy) solution. He says, "follow me." Jesus called to his disciples and one-by-one each followed. They could not have known what the journey would hold, or how their worlds would be turned upside-down by His presence.

They were radically transformed by following Jesus on their journey. He instructed them in the basics so they would later be able to invite others to follow them as they followed Christ. And not one of them would trade what they went through for the joy and rewards they received and are still enjoying as a result of their faithfulness.

Your call to follow is no less. He did not call you to keep you where you are but to radically transform you as you journey where He wants you to go. He promised He would never leave you or forsake you, and through His Spirit and His Word, He fulfills His promise to continue to lead you until your journey leads you home. It's the adventure of a lifetime! *Will you faithfully follow Jesus?*

HOW DO I CHANGE?

John 16:33, 1 Peter 1:6, 1 Peter 4:12

SELF-RULED
Approach to Trials/Suffering

Self-Examination
View of self/trial
based on desires,
fears, expectations,
or perceptions.
Romans 10:3
Proverbs 16:25

Unbiblical Response
Genesis 4:7

Practice Sin
John 8:34
1 John 3:7-9

Increased Problems
James 1:14-15

BONDAGE

Lack of hope. Lack of peace.
Lack of joy. Stress. Depression.
Anxiety. Addiction.

CHRIST-RULED
Approach to Trials/Suffering

Biblical Examination
View of self/trial based
on a biblical perspective.
2 Corinthians 13:5
Lamentations 3:40
Psalm 139:23

Biblical Response
2 Timothy 3:16-17

Practice Obedience
James 1:22-25
Ephesians 4:22-32

Increased Growth
2 Peter 3:18
Colossians 2:6-7

FREEDOM

Abundant blessings.
Abundant life. Peace.
Joy. Contentment.

151

APPENDICES

UNDERSTANDING MY SALVATION

Justified

Justification is God's instantaneous and irreversible declaration that the unrighteous are made positionally righteous (Romans 3:24-28; 4:1-5; 5:1-2). We are forever wrapped in the everlasting righteousness of Christ! His record becomes our record. His merit becomes our merit. From the moment of salvation, God treats us as righteous. Like His Son, we become God's children (1 John 3:1).

Sanctified

Sanctification is a progressive process that spans the believer's life. The ongoing work of the Spirit conforms the believer to the image of Jesus (Romans 8:29). This process happens in the ordinary circumstances and relationships of our daily lives as we put into practice living in dependence and obedience to God through his Word, the Bible (Colossians 3:16), and by his Spirit (Psalms 143:10, Romans 8:14).

I AM

Glorified

Glorification is a future hope, an event in which the believer will be fully completed and perfected in Christ at the final Resurrection (Romans 5:2; Colossians 1:27). At that time, our bodies are made new, and we are permanently separated from sin and all of its consequences (2 Thessalonians 2:14; 2 Timothy 2:10). In light of this truth we can endure the brokenness of this current life, recognizing that our pain and suffering are light and momentary compared to the Glory that is to come (2 Corinthians 4:17-18).

A BIBLICAL VIEW OF GOD

GOD IS

Perfect in Love

God demonstrates His love for us in that while we were still sinners, He gave His life for us (Romans 5:8). His sacrificial death on the cross as payment for our sins is the ultimate expression of love. In keeping with His nature, *He only does what is most loving for us* (Romans 8:37-39, 1 John 4 :9-11).

Infinite in Wisdom

God's wisdom is beyond our understanding. God doesn't just know and understand all things, He is the ultimate source of all wisdom and knowledge (Psalms 147:5, Romans 11:33). The Bible says that His thoughts are beyond our thoughts and that His ways are not our ways (Isaiah 55:8-9). In keeping with His nature *He always knows what is best for us.*

Completely Sovereign

God is the supreme authority and all things are under His control (Colossians 1:16). He will bring about what is most loving and *what He knows is best for us.*

RECOGNIZE-REPENT-REPLACE

RECOGNIZE

My thoughts and actions.
What do I need to "put off?"

"Let all bitterness and wrath and anger and clamor and slander be put away from you, along with all malice." –Ephesians 4:31

"But now you must put them all away: anger, wrath, malice, slander, and obscene talk from your mouth. Do not lie to one another, seeing that you have put off the old self with its practices." –Colossians 3:8-9

REPENT

Confess my sin, turn and walk in a new direction.
To change one's mind, walking away from
sin and towards God.

"If we confess our sins, he is faithful and just to forgive us our sins and to cleanse us from all unrighteousness." –1 John 1:9

REPLACE

God's thoughts and actions.
What do I need to "put on?"

"Put on then, as God's chosen ones, holy and beloved, compassionate hearts, kindness, humility, meekness, and patience, bearing with one another and, if one has a complaint against another, forgiving each other; as the Lord has forgiven you, so you also must forgive. And above all these put on love, which binds everything together in perfect harmony." –Colossians 3:12-14

WHO DOES GOD SAY I AM?

I AM

Forgiven (Psalm 32:1)

Redeemed (Galatians 3:13-14)

Rescued (Colossians 1:13-14)

Healed (Psalm 107:19-21)

Set Free (Galatians 5:1)

Chosen (1 Peter 2:9-10)

Sealed (Ephesians 1:13)

Sanctified (Hebrews 10:14)

Protected (2 Thessalonians 3:3)

Created in His Image (Genesis 1:27)

Transformed (2 Corinthians 3:18)

Rooted and Established (Colossians 2:6-7)

Adopted (Ephesians 1:5)

Fearfully and Wonderfully Made (Psalm 139:13-16)

His Ambassador (2 Corinthians 5:20)

Loved (1 John 4:10)

Taught, Reproved, Corrected and Trained (2 Timothy 3:16)

Disciplined (Hebrews 12:5-11)

Lavished With Grace (Ephesians 1:7-9)

Growing (2 Peter 3:18)

WHOSE KINGDOM?

SELF-RULED

You Become the Lawmaker

"Having begun by the Spirit, are you now being perfected by the flesh?…"
—Galatians 3:1-5

You Make Yourself Judge

"Judge not, that you be not judged. For with the judgment you pronounce you will be judged…"
—Matthew 7:1-5

You Dispense Punishment

"Behold, blessed is the one whom God reproves; therefore despise not the discipline of the Almighty."
—Job 5:17

BONDAGE

"Then desire when it has conceived gives birth to sin, and sin when it is fully grown brings forth death."
—James 1:15

CHRIST-RULED

Not Under the Law

"For by grace you have been saved…"
—Ephesians 2:8

Not Under Judgment or Condemnation

"There is therefore now no condemnation…"
—Romans 8:1

Not Deserving of Punishment and Death

"For the wages of sin is death, but the free gift of God is eternal life…"
—Romans 6:23

FREEDOM

"So if the Son sets you free, you will be free indeed."
—John 8:36

159

WHO RULES YOUR HEART?

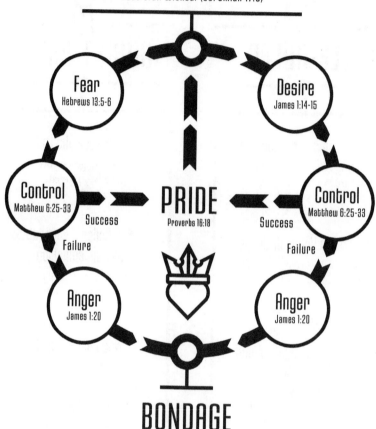

SELF-RULED
Deceitful. Wicked. (Jeremiah 17:9)

Fear
Hebrews 13:5-6

Desire
James 1:14-15

Control
Matthew 6:25-33

PRIDE
Proverbs 16:18

Control
Matthew 6:25-33

Success

Success

Failure

Failure

Anger
James 1:20

Anger
James 1:20

BONDAGE
Lack of hope. Lack of peace. Lack of joy. Regret. Depression. Anxiety. Addiction

Now the works of the flesh are evident: sexual immorality, impurity, sensuality, idolatry, sorcery, enmity, strife, jealousy, fits of anger, rivalries, dissensions, divisions, envy, drunkenness, orgies, and things like these. I warn you, as I warned you before, that those who do such things will not inherit the kingdom of God. —Galatians 5:19-21

WHO RULES YOUR HEART?

CHRIST-RULED

Christ lives in me. (Galatians 2:20)

Dependence
Proverbs 3:5-6

Obedience
James 1:22-25

Steadfastness
James 1:4

Peace
Philippians 4:6-7

Suffering/Trial
1 Peter 4:12-13

Suffering/Trial
1 Peter 4:12-13

Recognizing God's Control
Romans 8:28

Recognizing God's Control
Romans 8:28

FREEDOM

Hope. Peace. Joy. Forgiveness. Contentment.

But the fruit of the Spirit is love, joy, peace,
patience, kindness, goodness, faithfulness,
gentleness, self-control; against such
things there is no law. –Galatians 5:22-23

UNBIBLICAL THINKING
Part A

What influences how you think about your suffering?

Family, parent, coworker, neighbor, media, music, personal prejudices…

Describe the trial you are currently experiencing.

Explain how this trial affects you.

Conflict, finances, parenting, ability to function or think clearly,…

Note how this trial affects your feelings.

Feeling overwhelmed, wronged, hopeless, angry, fearful, numb, forgotten,…

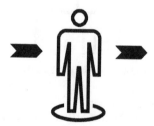

BIBLICAL THINKING
Part B

How does Biblical thinking change your view of your suffering?

Describe the trial you are currently experiencing.

Explain how biblical thinking affects you.

Note how biblical thinking affects your feelings.

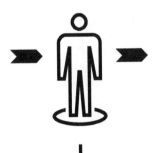

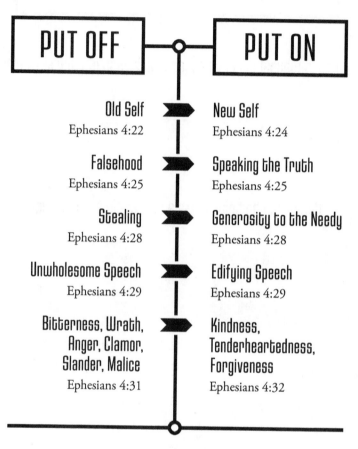

PUT OFF	PUT ON
Old Self Ephesians 4:22	New Self Ephesians 4:24
Falsehood Ephesians 4:25	Speaking the Truth Ephesians 4:25
Stealing Ephesians 4:28	Generosity to the Needy Ephesians 4:28
Unwholesome Speech Ephesians 4:29	Edifying Speech Ephesians 4:29
Bitterness, Wrath, Anger, Clamor, Slander, Malice Ephesians 4:31	Kindness, Tenderheartedness, Forgiveness Ephesians 4:32

Bitterness   Anger and disappointment at being treated unfairly; resentment.

Anger   A strong feeling of annoyance, displeasure, or hostility.

Rage/Wrath   Violent, uncontrolled anger.

Slander   The action or crime of making a false spoken statement damaging to a person's reputation.

Malice   The desire to harm someone; ill will.

HOW DO I CHANGE?

John 16:33, 1 Peter 1:6, 1 Peter 4:12

SELF-RULED
Approach to Trials/Suffering

Self-Examination

View of self/trial
based on desires,
fears, expectations,
or perceptions.
Romans 10:3
Proverbs 16:25

Unbiblical Response

Genesis 4:7

Practice Sin

John 8:34
1 John 3:7-9

Increased Problems

James 1:14-15

BONDAGE

Lack of hope. Lack of peace.
Lack of joy. Stress. Depression.
Anxiety. Addiction.

CHRIST-RULED
Approach to Trials/Suffering

Biblical Examination

View of self/trial based
on a biblical perspective.
2 Corinthians 13:5
Lamentations 3:40
Psalm 139:23

Biblical Response

2 Timothy 3:16-17

Practice Obedience

James 1:22-25
Ephesians 4:22-32

Increased Growth

2 Peter 3:18
Colossians 2:6-7

FREEDOM

Abundant blessings.
Abundant life. Peace.
Joy. Contentment.

DAILY PRACTICES

Be Spirit Led: Let the Spirit Control You

"And do not get drunk with wine, for that is debauchery, but be filled with the Spirit." –Ephesians 5:18

How are we filled with the Spirit? In the same way we are filled with alcohol. We drink it, we fill up our body with it and we come under its influence. On this journey we need the influence of God's Spirit that indwells us upon our salvation and serves as our guide. The Spirit instructs us in the direction we need to go in keeping with God's Word. The Spirit also gives us life: "For the bread of God is he who comes down from heaven and gives life to the world." –John 6:33

The Spirit produces evidence of His work in our heart: "But the fruit of the Spirit is love, joy, peace, patience, kindness, goodness, faithfulness, gentleness, self-control…" –Galatians 5:22-23a

Be Humble: Acknowledge God as God, and Yourself as Broken

"For thus says the One who is high and lifted up, who inhabits eternity, whose name is Holy: 'I dwell in the high and holy place, and also with him who is of a contrite and lowly spirit, to revive the spirit of the lowly, and to revive the heart of the contrite.'" —Isaiah 57:15

We can only acknowledge God to the extent that we know Him. When we know Him accurately, as He proclaims Himself through His Word, we can rightly exalt and lift Him high! Behold His wisdom, His mercy and His grace! Marvel at His character, as it is displayed on the pages of His Word and in the lives of His beloved image bearers.

Humility allows us to acknowledge our own brokenness (sinfulness), and lack of wisdom. Humility also leads us to recognize our need to depend on and to obey God for direction and grounding in truth.

The Bible instructs us to "take heed" to ourselves. This means examining our thinking, motives, and actions according to the manual God has given us: His Word. This will help us know if we are living in God's will, for His glory and our good!

Be Repentant: Turn from Sin

"Repent, for the kingdom of heaven is at hand." —Matthew 4:17

God's instruction manual, the Bible, states that He faithfully forgives our sins if we confess them (1 John 1:9). Confession acknowledges that our thoughts or actions contradict God's stated desires and expectations. Only God can deal with our sinful hearts. Our heart will always lead us to sin and destruction. God alone has the ability to create in us a pure or right heart and change our desires, so we can fully obey Him (Psalm 51:10).

Recognize—Repent—Replace

When we ***recognize*** that our thoughts or actions are off course (what the Bible calls sin), we are instructed to ***repent***: to confess our sin, turn and walk in a new direction, change our mind, walking away from sin and towards God. We then need to ***replace*** our rebellious and independent view with a right view of God in our lives. This daily—and sometimes moment by moment—practice that makes the journey viable and rewarding (see *Appendix C*).

Be in the Word: Meditate on God's Instruction Manual

"Let the word of Christ dwell in you richly…" –Colossians 3:16

God uses His Word to express and communicate Himself to us. He desires to be known. He set His own personal privacy aside and revealed Himself to His beloved children, to whom He sent His only son to save.

Our great and awesome God gives us His direction and guidance on how to live in this broken and fallen world. James warns that we should not just be ones who hear or read the Word but ones who also apply the Word (James 1:22).

Let God's Word thrill and exhilarate your soul. Marvel that the Living God, creator of the universe, is speaking to you! If you struggle to make reading the Word a priority, ask yourself if you have replaced God's truths with a lie. An inaccurate view of God will never draw you into His Word. Only the Holy Spirit can bring you closer to Himself as He communicates to you.

Be in Prayer: Talk & Listen to God

"Pray without ceasing." –1 Thessalonians 5:17

Prayer is simply talking to God. Because of what Christ did

for us on the cross, we have access to God the Father at all times! Even more awe-inspiring is His desire to have an open and loving relationship with us. How many times do we neglect or take for granted this great privilege and resource?

God wants to interact with us! He speaks to us chiefly through His Word, and we speak to Him through prayer. Sometimes we don't know how or what to pray, so praying God's Word is a great guide to developing a deeper prayer life.

Prayer is not just a means for us to ask God to orchestrate our lives, circumstances, and relationships in ways that make us feel better. Prayer brings our will into line with God's will and Word. Remember, He is committed to walking us through our deepest problem, our brokenness and our sin. He will orchestrate circumstances and relationships in ways that refine our faith and reflect His character. Pray for God to continue to work in your life regardless of what difficulties or suffering you face.

Prayer is also a means of rejoicing in who our great God and Savior is. Enjoy your time with Him continually.

Be in Community: Spend Time with God's People

"For just as the body is one and has many members, and all the members of the body, though many, are one body, so it is with Christ. For in one Spirit we were all baptized into one body..."
–1 Corinthians 12:12-13a

God saved us into His Kingdom and covered us under His righteous reign. But look around! He did not place you or me in His Kingdom alone. Others, who also have been saved by His grace and are on the journey of spiritual growth, surround us. He not only gave us Himself, but He gave us each other. We are to come together to encourage and spur one another on to love and good deeds. (Hebrews 10:24)

We all need people in our lives who will point us back to the true God and ruler of our hearts. We are also called to serve one another and to bear one another's burdens within authentic community. Upon salvation, God gives each of us gifts meant to encourage and equip the body (church) for the work of reaching others with the Gospel! When we seek out relationships from different age groups and backgrounds, we all win. Authentic relationships with a variety of others within the community of believers create opportunities to show our love for and obedience to God. Let us join together in humble submission to one another for this journey as we learn to live in the great Kingdom of God.

Be Worshipful: Glorify God with Everything

"Rejoice in the Lord always..." –Philippians 4:4

Worship flows out of thinking rightly about who God is and exalting Him continually in our thoughts and actions. We sometimes think of worship as limited to singing in a Sunday morning church service, but that is a narrow and shallow view of what the Bible describes as worship. We are called to worship the Lord with all our heart, soul and mind. Worship, therefore, encompasses everything we do in life.

If our view of God is one of our own making we will never worship Him with whole hearts. We must bring our desires, our will, and our thinking, into submission to the God of the universe. If we are not exalting and worshiping Him, we will exalt and worship ourselves. Instead, let's practice being a worshiper of God and God alone.

Be His Image Bearer: Reveal God to the World

"Therefore be imitators of God…" –Ephesians 5:1

As people redeemed and reconciled by the blood of Jesus, we are now able to bear His image to the world around us. To be like Jesus, then, means being a living explanation of God to a broken and lost world. As servants of His kingdom, we are to proclaim Him, and replicate the Christian life in all who believe. We are to go wherever God calls us and to share the good news of the Gospel of His grace and love. He has tasked us with no less than teaching all who believe to live in obedience to Christ the King. Our mission is to build His kingdom, share His story, and to bear His image, for His glory, inviting others on the journey!

IN THE GRIP OF GLORY

The Gospel for Everyday Living
By Chara Donahue

For He is Glorious

God's ways are higher than my own. His thoughts, like the heavens, are beyond my comprehension.[1]

He existed before creation[2] and crafted the universe from nothing.[3] He sets the boundary lines for the oceans,[4] and commands where lightning should strike.[5] By His breath the starry host emerged.[6]

---

[1] Isaiah 55:9 "For as the heavens are higher than the earth, so are my ways higher than your ways and my thoughts than your thoughts."

[2] Psalm 90:2 "Before the mountains were brought forth, or ever you had formed the earth and the world, from everlasting to everlasting you are God."

[3] Genesis 1:1 "In the beginning, God created the heavens and the earth."

[4] Job 38:11 "And said, 'Thus far shall you come, and no farther, and here shall your proud waves be stayed.'"

[5] Job 36:32 "He covers his hands with the lightning and commands it to strike the mark."

[6] Psalm 33:6 "By the word of the Lord the heavens were made, and by the breath of his mouth all their host."

He embodies greatness, goodness, and all that is holy[7] pouring out mercy and distributing justice perfectly and precisely.[8]

He is the bringer of all that is good.[9] Every moment, step, and heartbeat is given by Him.[10] I rest in the truth that He is in control of all things.[11]

Hurt, despair, and terror try to creep in and conquer those He created,[12] but He cannot be overcome. He is the light shining in the darkness.[13]

This God, the true God, the only God, is worthy of all praise.[14]

He has allowed me to delight in His presence and glory.[15] I seek Him out for He sought me,[16] so I may delight as I offer him my obedience as an act of love.[17]

Created in His image,[18] I have the privilege of living to glorify Him, as one reconciled to Him by His great love.[19]

---

[7] Isaiah 57:15 "For thus says the One who is high and lifted up, who inhabits eternity, whose name is Holy..."

[8] Ephesians 2:4 "But God, being rich in mercy, because of the great love with which he loved us," Psalm 9:8 "And he judges the world with righteousness; he judges the peoples with uprightness."

[9] James 1:17 "Every good gift and every perfect gift is from above, coming down from the Father of lights, with whom there is no variation or shadow due to change."

[10] Job 12:10 "In his hand is the life of every living thing and the breath of all mankind."

[11] Isaiah 45:11-12 "Thus says the Lord, the Holy One of Israel, and the one who formed him: 'Ask me of things to come; will you command me concerning my children and the work of my hands? I made the earth and created man on it; it was my hands that stretched out the heavens, and I commanded all their host.'"

[12] Isaiah 25:8 "He will swallow up death forever; and the LORD God will wipe away tears from all faces, and the reproach of his people he will take away from all the earth, for the Lord has spoken."

[13] John 1:5 "The light shines in the darkness, and the darkness has not overcome it."

[14] Isaiah 44:6 "Thus says the Lord, the King of Israel and his Redeemer, the Lord of hosts: 'I am the first and I am the last; besides me there is no god.'"

[15] Psalm 16:11 "You make known to me the path of life; in your presence there is fullness of joy; at your right hand are pleasures forevermore."

[16] Isaiah 62:12 "And they shall be called The Holy People, The Redeemed of the Lord; and you shall be called Sought Out, A City Not Forsaken."

[17] 2 John 1:6 "And this is love, that we walk according to his commandments; this is the commandment, just as you have heard from the beginning, so that you should walk in it."

[18] Genesis 1:27 "So God created man in his own image, in the image of God he created him; male and female he created them."

[19] 2 Corinthians 5:19 "That is, in Christ God was reconciling the world to himself, not counting their trespasses against them, and entrusting to us the message of reconciliation."

I Have Fallen Short of Glory

Yet I gave in to the seduction of temporary pleasure and the call of instant gratification. I exchanged His truth for a lie and bowed down to worship my own wants, desires, and lusts,[20] falling short of all that He has created me to be.[21]

Instead of resting in His truth—trusting that He is who He says He is—I chose me. I knelt down to puny altars of my own creation that failed and brought me into affliction and sorrow.[22]

I viewed His great commandments as suggestions, picking and choosing which I would follow. I flaunted my wisdom, but was clearly the fool.[23]

Following my ways led me nowhere, but further from my God and closer to Hell.[24]

Apart from Christ I am without redemption. Without mercy.[25] Revealed for all that I am—a desperate, self-serving slave to sin wallowing in shame and my own demise.[26] Unable to approach His throne, I face an eternity separated from Him. Torn from all that is good and holy, I am left to darkness, left to the stain of sin. A soul destined for eternal torment.[27]

---

[20] Romans 1:21-25 "For although they knew God, they did not honor him as God or give thanks to him, but they became futile in their thinking, and their foolish hearts were darkened. Claiming to be wise, they became fools, and exchanged the glory of the immortal God for images resembling mortal man and birds and animals and creeping things. Therefore God gave them up in the lusts of their hearts to impurity, to the dishonoring of their bodies among themselves, because they exchanged the truth about God for a lie and worshiped and served the creature rather than the Creator, who is blessed forever! Amen."

[21] Romans 3:23 "For all have sinned and fall short of the glory of God,"

[22] Amos 2:4b "Because they have rejected the law of the LORD, and have not kept his statutes, but their lies have led them astray, those after which their fathers walked."

[23] 1 Corinthians 3:19 "For the wisdom of this world is folly with God. For it is written, "HE CATCHES THE WISE IN THEIR CRAFTINESS," (emphasis added)

[24] Matthew 25:46 "And these will go away into eternal punishment, but the righteous into eternal life."

[25] 1 Peter 2:10 "Once you were NOT A PEOPLE, but now you are GOD'S PEOPLE; once you had NOT RECEIVED MERCY, but now you have RECEIVED MERCY." (emphasis added)

[26] John 8:34 "Jesus answered them, 'Truly, truly, I say to you, everyone who practices sin is a slave to sin.'"

[27] Matthew 13:49-50 "'So it will be at the end of the age. The angels will come out and separate the evil from the righteous and throw them into the fiery furnace. In that place there will be weeping and gnashing of teeth.'"

The Glory of Grace

God stepped in—descended from His throne in Heaven and entered earth as a baby.[28]

As the God-man Jesus Christ, He rescued and redeemed what no man could. The Father sent His son, the firstborn over all creation[29] as the perfect sacrifice to save the people in a dying world.[30]

Those people then crucified the Son of God, but I might as well have been the one driving the nails. My sins were paid for, by an act of love like no other.[31] A love willing to suffer and die.[32] The one love that's willing to lay down life so others may know life eternally.[33]

God suffered the loss of His son, who became wholeness and redemption to all who come by faith.[34]

He removed the stain that deeply marked my soul and makes me clean.[35]

He's the Prince of Peace[36] who took what I deserved as he suffered and died on the cross.

For me he was mocked. For His Church he was crucified.[37]

---

[28] Luke 2:11 "For unto you is born this day in the city of David a Savior, who is Christ the Lord."
[29] Colossians 1:15 "He is the image of the invisible God, the firstborn of all creation."
[30] John 3:16 "'For God so loved the world, that he gave his only Son, that whoever believes in him should not perish but have eternal life.'"
[31] Colossians 2:13-14 "And you, who were dead in your trespasses and the uncircumcision of your flesh, God made alive together with him, having forgiven us all our trespasses, by canceling the record of debt that stood against us with its legal demands. This he set aside, nailing it to the cross."
[32] John 15:13-14 "Greater love has no one than this, that someone lay down his life for his friends. You are my friends if you do what I command you."
[33] John 10:10-11 "The thief comes only to steal and kill and destroy. I came that they may have life and have it abundantly. I am the good shepherd. The good shepherd lays down his life for the sheep."
[34] 1 Corinthians 1:30 "And because of him[a] you are in Christ Jesus, who became to us wisdom from God, righteousness and sanctification and redemption,"
[35] Isaiah 1:18 "Come now, let us reason together, says the LORD: though your sins are like scarlet, they shall be as white as snow; though they are red like crimson, they shall become like wool."
[36] Isaiah 9:6b "...And his name shall be called Wonderful Counselor, Mighty God, Everlasting Father, Prince of Peace."
[37] Matthew 27:31 "And when they had mocked him, they stripped him of the robe and put his own clothes on him and led him away to crucify him."

For His beloved He was buried.[38] For those who would have been rejected He arose![39]

He conquered death so that those who came to Him would not taste horror but rest in holy peace and everlasting joy.[40]

The soul is eternal; the body is but a temporary dwelling.[41] He came so that life in this body is not the best there ever is.[42]

His own are rescued from the torment that awaits those who reject Him time and time again.[43]

The hope of Heaven empowers the soul to press on, go into the world, and share the love.[44]

The love overflows from my heart, for I am loved. Perfectly, deeply, and truly by Him who sees all but loves me still.[45]

He has adopted me as His own. A child heir to the kingdom of Heaven.[46]

I've been given the Holy Spirit as a constant companion, comforter, and counselor, who reminds me of truth when it is needed, and helps me know that I will not be left or forsaken even when all my limited sight sees is the world's darkness.[47]

I am free—no longer a slave to the sin that led me to disaster

---

[38] John 19:41-42 "Now in the place where he was crucified there was a garden, and in the garden a new tomb in which no one had yet been laid. So because of the Jewish day of Preparation, since the tomb was close at hand, they laid Jesus there."

[39] Mark 16:6 "And he said to them, "Do not be alarmed. You seek Jesus of Nazareth, who was crucified. He has risen; he is not here. See the place where they laid him.""

[40] Isaiah 25:8 "He will swallow up death forever; and the Lord God will wipe away tears from all faces, and the reproach of his people he will take away from all the earth, for the LORD has spoken."

[41] 2 Corinthians 5:1 "For we know that if the tent that is our earthly home is destroyed, we have a building from God, a house not made with hands, eternal in the heavens."

[42] 1 Corinthians 15:53 "For this perishable body must put on the imperishable, and this mortal body must put on immortality."

[43] John 12:48 "The one who rejects me and does not receive my words has a judge; the word that I have spoken will judge him on the last day."

[44] Philippians 3:14 "I press on toward the goal for the prize of the upward call of God in Christ Jesus."

[45] 1 John 4:16 "So we have come to know and to believe the love that God has for us. God is love, and whoever abides in love abides in God, and God abides in him."
Hebrews 4:13: "And no creature is hidden from his sight, but all are naked and exposed to the eyes of him to whom we must give account."

[46] Galatians 4:7 "So you are no longer a slave, but a son, and if a son, then an heir through God."

[47] John 14:16 "And I will ask the Father, and he will give you another Helper, to be with you forever,"

and pain. I've been given the Spirit's gift of self-control and peace.[48] For goodness and mercy follow me even in valleys of sorrow and death.[49]

All trial and troubles will be worked together for good by my God.[50]

When I fail, His wrath does not fall on me, but gentle correction and comfort comes to me.[51]

His desire is to let forgiveness cover all I have done and will do.[52]

When I come to Him in confession, He meets me in my brokenness, and shows me how I can turn from my sin[53] and find hope, faith, and love.[54]

He wishes for me to live the abundant life of abiding in His love, and He is grieved by the times I turn my back on Him.[55]

Yet He awaits my return with open arms, and draws me deeper into His heart.[56]

He is God, and I am His.[57]

---

[48] Galatians 5:1 "For freedom Christ has set us free; stand firm therefore, and do not submit again to a yoke of slavery."
Galatians 5:22-23 "But the fruit of the Spirit is love, joy, peace, patience, kindness, goodness, faithfulness, gentleness, self-control; against such things there is no law."

[49] Psalm 23:6 "Surely goodness and mercy shall follow me all the days of my life, and I shall dwell in the house of the Lord forever."

[50] Romans 8:28 "And we know that for those who love God all things work together for good, for those who are called according to his purpose."

[51] 1 Thessalonians 1:10 "And to wait for his Son from heaven, whom he raised from the dead, Jesus who delivers us from the wrath to come."

[52] Acts 3:19-20b "Repent therefore, and turn back, that your sins may be blotted out, that times of refreshing may come from the presence of the Lord…"

[53] 1 John 1:9 "If we confess our sins, he is faithful and just to forgive us our sins and to cleanse us from all unrighteousness."

[54] 1 Corinthians 13:13 "So now faith, hope, and love abide, these three; but the greatest of these is love."

[55] Colossians 1:13-14 "He has delivered us from the domain of darkness and transferred us to the kingdom of his beloved Son, in whom we have redemption, the forgiveness of sins."

[56] John 1:12 "But to all who did receive him, who believed in his name, he gave the right to become children of God,"

[57] Psalm 100:3 "Know that the LORD, he is God! It is he who made us, and we are his; we are his people, and the sheep of his pasture."